AN ERK AMONG THE ELKS

By the same author:

1906 Accident on the Railway at Grantham
Traction Engines, Shire Publications
Farming with Steam, Shire Publications
Smoke and Steam
Saga of the Steam Plough (2nd Edition), David and Charles
Traction Engines, Robert Tyndall

AN ERK AMONG THE ELKS

Harold Bonnett

Harold Bonnett
4.12.1998

The Book Guild Ltd
Sussex, England

This book is sold subject to the condition that it shall not, by way of trade or otherwise, be lent, re-sold, hired out, photocopied or held in any retrieval system or otherwise circulated without the publisher's prior consent in any form of binding or cover other than that in which this is published and without a similar condition including this condition being imposed on the subsequent purchaser.

The Book Guild Ltd
25 High Street,
Lewes, Sussex

First published 1998
© Harold Bonnett 1998
Set in Times

Typesetting by Wordset
Hassocks, West Sussex

Printed in Great Britain by
Bookcraft (Bath) Ltd,
Avon

A catalogue record for this book is
available from the British Library

ISBN 1 85776 288 6

Erk *– an ordinary aircraftman, having neither stripes nor commission*

(RAF slang)

CONTENTS

	Prologue – When War Broke Out . . .	ix
1	Overseas Journey	1
2	No. 38 Service Flying Training School	5
3	The Estevan Countryside	8
4	The Airfield Begins to Lick Itself into Shape	10
5	Plane Crashes and an Overturned Tractor	14
6	Farming and General	16
7	Visits to the USA	19
8	Progress of the War	27
9	No. 38 SFTS Gets into its Stride	29
10	A Wet Saturday Afternoon	33
11	A Look at the Rocky Mountains	35
12	No. 38 SFTS Carries on with its Training Programme	50
13	A Forced Landing in the USA	53
14	Winter Weather and Discipline	57
15	Christmas in Canada 1942	59
16	The War Situation in 1943	62
17	Catching up on Delays due to Christmas Leave and Snowfalls	64
18	A Likeable Chap who was an Incorrigible Rogue	67

19	Wild Flowers, Animals and Wild Fruit	69
20	Miscellaneous Matters	72
21	A Snow Blizzard	74
22	The Flood that Followed theSnowstorm	76
23	In Hospital	78
24	More Pressure on the Workload at Estevan	80
25	The Opening up of Western Canada, and the Native Americans	82
26	More about Flying in the RAF	86
27	Odds and Ends	88
28	By Train and Hitch-hiking to Los Angeles and Back	92
29	Back to the Work of Winning the War	105
30	Progress of the War, late 1943	108
31	Farms and Countryside	111
32	Work, Deserters and Crime	115
33	Events at the End of 1943	119
34	My Last Weeks at No. 38 S.F.T.S. Estevan	123
35	A Posting to Penhold	127
36	Vancouver Island	131
37	Vancouver and Jasper Park	139
38	Alberta Snippets	142
39	A Look at the Alaska Highway	151
40	Homeward-bound	157

Epilogue – Back to the Job   161

PROLOGUE

When War Broke Out

When war broke out in 1939, I was employed as a clerk in the office of the locomotive department of the London and North Eastern Railway at March in Cambridgeshire. In May 1940 I was married to my wife, Hilda, during the week that the Germans smashed up the French army and invaded France.

Early in 1941 I was called to the recruitment office in Cambridge and after a medical examination I was told that I was going into the army when I was called up. I wanted to go into the RAF and when I showed that I knew how to test a carburettor float for leaks, it was agreed that I should be accepted for training as a flight mechanic.

Whilst waiting for my call-up we had several visits from low-flying German raiding aircraft, both in the town of March and along its railway lines. One German aircraft shot up, head on, the locomotive working from Spalding to March; the driver brought the engine outside our office and showed us how one bullet had pierced the half-inch thick boiler plate of the engine's dome. There was a long straight stream of escaping steam impinging on the engine's chimney.

I was in the Home Guard and at first took my rifle to the office. I also had a khaki battledress and a service gas mask. Other war work was, along with another clerk in the office named Arthur Steel, to do a spell of night watching at the entrance of the loco department premises, and also alongside the signal box at the departure end of the large Whitemoor freight yard. We also did some rifle training practice at the Upwood aerodrome about ten miles away.

I was called up in the autumn of 1941, passed through the reception depot at Cardington near Bedford, where I was put into uniform and sent for about six weeks square bashing at Bournemouth and then sent to the RAF mechanical training centre at Halton in Buckinghamshire to be trained as a flight mechanic on aero engines. This lasted for about six weeks. I was then sent to Coningsby Airfield in Lincolnshire, where they had quite a few of a new type of bomber known as Manchesters. These planes were equipped with a new type of Rolls Royce engine that had four banks of cylinders arranged in the form of an X, and they were not performing very well. One engine that I was told to inspect and repair had almost every exhaust screening plate bolt with stripped threads in the cylinder block, apparently due to the vibration of these engines. I could not find sufficient metal to hold a new set of threads. I think that shortly afterwards these planes were withdrawn.

In the month of March I was informed that I was posted for overseas leave, and given two weeks' leave. My wife was not too pleased to hear of this, but knew that dozens of other men's wives were faced with the loss of a husband, so we took a week's holiday in Torquay and thoroughly enjoyed it.

I reported back at Coningsby and in two or three days I was on my way by train to Blackpool, where overseas drafts were rekitted, and sent to the boat.

1

Overseas Journey

One morning early in April 1942, as the troop train in which I had travelled all night from Blackpool to Glasgow passed along the south bank of the river Clyde, we had a touching send-off from about fifty Scots women who hung from their windows waving flags or towels. They did not know more than that this was just another train load of troops of some sort or other who were on their way overseas, but they certainly sent their best wishes. I must say that the scene brought a couple of tears into my eyes.

About three evenings later, as it grew dark, the *Batory*, a Polish-built and owned ship now requisitioned by the British Government, slipped quietly from her midstream moorings and crept westwards. There were about 300 of us in an RAF draft of ground personnel on board and, while we did not know where we were off to, rumour was that as we had handed in our gas masks it seemed very likely that the destination was Canada. Whatever the future held for me, I knew that I had no say in the matter, so I would treat it all as an adventure.

As I leaned over the deck handrails, the ship passed many dark objects.

My daydreams were cut short by a tap on my shoulder by an RAF corporal, who demanded, 'Name and number?' He jotted down my answer and said, 'Report to No. 2 anti-aircraft gun position at 11.00 p.m. until 3.00 a.m., and again at 10.00 a.m.'

This shook me and I immediately replied, 'I have never fired an anti-aircraft gun in my life.'

He replied, 'Never mind about that because if anything happens a gunner will be there.

And that was that.

Shortly afterwards the ship approached what looked like a dark barrier across the river, with shaded red lights indicating a narrow central passage through what looked like a submarine obstacle. I spent the night all alone, sitting in the base of the anti-aircraft gun. Meanwhile the pace of the ship quickened and at the same time she began to plunge and roll quite a bit. By the time that I was relieved at 3.00 a.m. I had begun to feel a little seasick.

At 10.00 a.m. when I took duty again, I felt miserable with seasickness. However, it was a lovely morning with the sun shining brilliantly as it lit up the ocean in front of us. What a splendid seascape there was ahead and I had a wonderful open view of it from my elevated position on the port side of the captain's deck. It was plain to see that we were in company with another ship about the size of the *Batory* and that both ships were being escorted by two USA four-funnelled Lend-Lease destroyers that lay one on each side of the small convoy. There was not another ship to be seen. On the bow deck below there were some German prisoners of war taking exercise. Immediately the thought entered my mind that the German secret service would know that these men were with us and that they would not attempt to torpedo us.

As the gun turret was located on the port side of the captain's bridge deck, he was in full view of me as he strode to and fro, hands clasped behind him.

He stopped, looked at me and rather sharply snapped out, 'Airman, look to your duty. You are a lookout man for enemy aircraft which may now have a long range over the Atlantic. Your life and mine, may depend on you. Look all the time at the sky.'

That put me in my place all right. During the second day out, the weather turned colder and the sea somewhat rougher, due, I think, to our course being set somewhat north-west. We had the usual drills in what to do if any alarms were sounded. We had to put on lifebelts and assemble at fixed points on the deck. At evening on the second day we slipped the dead body of someone who had died on board into the depths of the Atlantic. The scene of the sea burial reminded my very much of Turner's painting, 'Burial at Sea'. We slept in hammocks on board ship. That day I was told that my anti-aircraft gun duties were at an end, because we were now out of the range of enemy aircraft.

Late on the second day out a gale blew up and during the night the sea became mountainous, causing us to be confined below decks. In the morning it was seen that several deck structures had been washed away. All that was left of a row of temporary lavatories were the stubs of the lavatory bowls. However, we had, so far, been free from submarine alarms. The sea waves were still high, but I could not make out what the dark and small objects were that darted across the troughs between the crests and seemed to disappear into the dark mass of each rising wall of water. They seemed to be small birds, a little larger than wrens. I had read of seabirds which the sailors called Mother Carey's chickens, but I may never know the answer.

Then, quite suddenly, the sirens sounded an alarm, and we had all to put on our life jackets and assemble at our danger stations. I could see that our two escorting destroyers had dropped behind and were doing circles, whilst dropping depth charges that threw up fountains of water. Almost immediately the all-clear sounded. All that we were told afterwards was that the sonar equipment had detected nothing more than a shoal of very large fish.

It was on the next day that a land bird settled on the ship's rigging, and soon we saw a lowish line of cliffs in front of us. We landed at Halifax. On the same day we were disembarked and taken by train to Monkton, a transit camp about six or seven miles away. We were there only a few days, but what lovely meals they gave us – bacon and fried eggs for breakfast, and so on. I think that it was on the Saturday evening that we were marched to the station and loaded on to a special train. We were told that it would be a journey of about three to four days to some place on the western prairies of Canada.

At about 6.00 a.m. next morning there was a nasty bump and a sudden stop that woke us all up. A flight sergeant came along the train telling us that there had been a slight accident of some sort or other and that it would be some time before the train could go forward. About half an hour afterwards we were told that it would be some hours before the train could go on. Meanwhile, those who wished could get out for exercise. There was a little wooden hut alongside the line at the front end of the train, a small cafe or shop that would be opened shortly – hot coffee and light bites would be available. I was one of those that got out. Everywhere it was a white world, covered in snow.

The accident had been caused by two trains being allowed to be on the same single line, one going east and ours westward bound, with the result that the two locomotives had met head-on. The locomotive of our train had suffered the most damage, for its cylindrical water tank had been squeezed up like a concertina. The site of the mishap had been either at or near a place called Rivière du Loup (Wolf River). It was almost midday before we got going again. Between 5.00 and 6.00 p.m. I seem to remember that we stopped at some small place where a meal had been laid on for us.

Two days later we passed over countryside that had less snow on it. We also ran along the north shore of Lake Superior, where the railway passed under quite steep cliffs. The train stopped for a few moments and the sun shone quite brightly. A large brown butterfly was sunning itself on the face of the smooth rocks; it was the first wild creature that I had seen in Canada.

Our train journey finished during the next day at Estevan, a small prairie town in Saskatchewan, some 100 miles south of Regina and about six miles north of the Canada and USA boundary. The name Saskatchewan is a derivative of a Native American word that means 'a swift flowing river'.

2

No.38 Service Flying Training School

A brand new airfield, of soundly constructed wooden buildings with three tarmacadamized runways and six hangars, were all ready for us to occupy. A few aircraft were already flying. The last of the runways was at the point of being finished. An American steam roller, now fitted with an internal combustion engine, was doing its last runs. On the second day after our arrival we started work. Practically all the aircraft were British Anson IIs, fitted with American-built Jacobs radial seven-cylinder engines.

It was of course, under the Commonwealth Air Training Plan, at a cost of $3 million Can. that No.38 Service Flying Training School was established. At one time in 1943 there were no fewer than 256 trainee pilots on the station. At another unspecified time there were some 1,800 officers and men at the airfield.

The land on which the airfield was built was sandy and had not been very fertile to the first farmers. Many farms had already been deserted and the only traces of the homesteads were a few rhubarb clumps, or bits of garden windbreaks in the form of a yellow flowering bush called carragoner. According to what local people told us, the first settlers, mostly American, had a practice of living in California. In spring they came up to Canada, planted crops of wheat or barley, threshed it on the fields, sold the grain in September or October, before getting on to special trains back to California where they spent a carefree winter. After several years of such rough farming the land became exhausted and, discouraged by several drought-ridden summers, these early settlers sold out.

The purpose of No.38 SFTS was to give trainee pilots who had already received elementary tuition on such small machines as Gypsy Moths, the experience of larger machines. With this purpose in mind, we all set to work. Some of the planes that were actually flying were kept in hangars that also undertook light maintenance repairs. I was put into the servicing side, looking after the planes that did the daily flying. Each morning we had to push out the planes, check that their tanks were full of petrol, and run up the engines to the required r.p.m. We saw each plane off and ran out to direct each plane as it came in to a place on the tarmac. Flying started at about 8.00 a.m. and went on until 7.00 p.m. It was our job to wheel in the planes for the night, but before we could finish work we had to give each plane a stipulated daily inspection and sign for it. Sometimes it was about 8.00 p.m. before we finished work. In order to avoid too long a working day, there was often an early and a late shift. Generally speaking the weather was fine enough for flying to continue all day, but there were exceptions. Heavy rain, dust storms, smoke from distant burning prairie grass or the setting alight of the previous season's heaps of threshed straw by the farmers, or in winter when snow fell – all of these things could put a stop to flying.

A fair number of the flying instructors were men who had done long periods of flying under battle conditions in Europe and were having a rest period.

Corporal Hall told me that I had been given the charge of plane No. 8562 and this suited me fine because I much preferred having my own plane to look after. However, this arrangement soon fell through – but I was given No. 8430 a few weeks later.

Very soon it was found that odd chaps were standing about, and although this was in many cases simply because they were quick workers, the officers seized on this to have a situation where we were all running at our work.

Group Captain Cummings, the station C.O. caught Squib Brown and two other mechanics smoking in the lavatories of 'F' Flight. The punishment for this was three days 'Jankers', which meant that they had to report at 6.00 a.m. each morning to the guard room police, who gave them any old job that wanted doing.

It was not before very long that many of the airmen started to complain about being in Canada. There was a rumour that, at a station well to our west, there had been a general walkout of the RAF personnel. Certainly our food was better than it had been in England, but of course sometimes careless washing up in the airmen's mess meant that there was food left on the cutlery and so on. Generally speaking, for myself I felt that things were not too bad. Another thing, too, was that whenever a complaint of any kind was made, something was usually done to find a remedy. At first we did not have a cinema, but very soon there was a nightly film show in the drill hall and many of us took advantage of two or three nights a week at the pictures.

Although I must admit that what suited me did not appeal to most airmen. I considered that a 48 hour weekend leave once a month, and two weeks' annual leave, were good allowances. Travel facilities were in no way restricted, neither did we need passports for going into the USA. Later on, the Canadian government, in an attempt to limit the amount of Canadian currency that was spent in the USA, stipulated that airmen wishing to visit the USA must obtain an invitation showing that the people they were visiting would treat them as guests. This stipulation was followed soon afterwards by a limit of a few Canadian dollars that could be taken into the USA. Although hindrances to travel, these restrictions could easily be overcome.

Early in 1942 the RAF introduced an arrangement whereby airmen's wives could come out and join their husbands in Canada. Since it meant that these wives had to pay most of the cost of the outward journey and all the return travel, and since there was at that time no living-out allowance for RAF men, only a few of the wives came out.

3

The Estevan Countryside

If you stood and cast your eyes around the countryside outside the airfield boundaries you had a wide view of open country, made up mostly of prairie farmlands. There were mild undulations here and there, but it was only across the south, about 10 or 20 miles away in North Dakota, USA, that there were any hills above 100 feet. The only tall trees were in the valley of the Souris river, that had cut its way down 30 or 40 feet into the land surface. As far as the distant horizon it was generally flattish farmlands or, where the land was not fertile, there were large clumps of wild bush. Very few of the farmers' fields had fences, neither were there always hedges or fences along the roadsides.

The settlers' farmsteads stood on the farmers' lands. The houses were of wooden construction and there was inevitably a large wooden barn that was the largest of all the farm buildings, usually painted red. It was usual practice to have a steel-framed windmill that pumped up water and perhaps generated some electricity for the farmstead. These windmills could be seen from the air whilst we were flying, with their sails spinning merrily.

About a hundred yards from the airfield entrance there was a little wooden hut known as Stella's. She had set up with it as a small cafe in order to cater for the contractors who built the airfield. She carried on with the cafe business and it served as a place where the airmen could get off the camp for a change of meals.

At Estevan we were off the main highways and even the road to Regina, capital of Saskatchewan, was surfaced with rough gravel. The use of the large scraper machines to lift back the gravel onto the road centres left shallow ditches at the sides of most roads. In winter, of course, all these roadways were frozen rock hard. A branch line of the Canadian Pacific Railway passed through Estevan and it was a single line. About ten miles east there was a branch line that ran south towards Portal on the USA border, to connect with what they called the 'Soo Line', so named because it passed through country formerly occupied by the Sioux tribe of Native Americans. The CPR had a small locomotive exchange point on the Canadian side of the border, because the USA engines did not run into Canada. On one of my early hitch-hiking days out I went to look at this site, staying in the hotel that had been a fine place in the early days, but was now looking very dilapidated and had few customers. I went out from the hotel and walked over to the railway where a CPR man was in charge – I think he was graded as a steam raiser. A big Pacific-type locomotive with a 4-6-2 wheel arrangement was in the yard and this man showed me many of its features. It had a wide firegrate, with rocking bars to drop clinker into the ashpan. It was loaded with rather small coal that was taken into the firebox by a mechanical stoker that used steam jets to blow the coal onto all parts of the firebox firegrate. I noticed that the wheel tyres of this engine were badly worn down and in fact they had fairly deep grooves in them.

Shortly afterwards I met a section man who told me that he had emigrated from Poland in 1914 when Austria had annexed his part of Poland. This man has some connection with maintenance of the rail track and said that where wooden sleepers were used, those made of birchwood lasted about 25 years.

About six or seven miles east of Estevan there was a little coal mining carried out. This brown coal, or lignite, was found under a clay cover about 20 feet deep and actually this clay was a deposit of the ice age when glaciers covered this part of Canada. The coal was in seams 10 to 12 feet thick and lifts took the miners down to the coal. This low grade coal was fetched by farmers and householders, who paid about $1.25 (28p) a ton for it. Some of the coal was taken away by rail. I rather think that this coal was used to fire the heating boilers in our RAF No.38 SFTS.

4

The Airfield Begins to Lick Itself into Shape

One June evening in 1942 we had quite an argument in our barrack room. It was all about discipline, when I said that Brown and Broadbank should have waited in the camp cinema to stand for the national anthem, instead of slipping out by a side door. At lights out it was still going on, although it was now down to whether discipline in the German army was better than it was in the British army. Later on in the war a small section of the airmen began to regard Stalin as a leader with a very humane outlook. Time, however, proved this to be a fallacy.

As I came back from tea, a warrant officer bawled out at me for attempting to enter the sergeants' mess, which was always out of bounds to ordinary airmen. All I wanted to do was to buy a newspaper from the man selling them inside the door.

Two corporals, Oldbury (in charge of parachutes) and Napper (blacksmith and welder), had beds next to mine. They liked their drink. One night they came in from the canteen very drunk and were sick all over the floor. Napper was put to bed, but got up again to argue furiously some point or other with Nobby Clark and Don Jennings.

Periodically we airmen were chased up – Sergeant Lowe told us that a new warrant officer named Green would not stand any idling by mechanics. Any spare time must be devoted to cleaning aircraft. It must be said, however, that our corporals and sergeants treated us with considerable civility. Whenever we had any engine problems, these NCOs were quick to give us guidance.

One day I asked Flight Sergeant Robinson, a pupil, if I could fly with him in Anson 8430. He said only if I had Flight Sergeant

Lowe's permission. This seemed a bit tough, because other chaps had done quite a lot of flying without permission.

On 16 July 1942 a sudden and violent storm blew in from the west. Sheets of rain swept along like smoke and everywhere was drenched. Lightning flashed all the time, but there was no hail with it. The intense wind blew over several planes, whilst others were lifted off their picketing posts. One aircraft was turned completely on its back and one of its main planes was broken off. One could never tell what oddities of summer weather would be likely to turn up.

The quality of the cookhouse food varied from time to time. One day we had beef and potatoes for dinner, but, like most Canadian beef, it was tough. I left it on my plate, but was able to make up for this by taking two helpings of raisin tart that was more to my liking. In the early spring, when the wild onions shot up their stems in the prairie grass, they were eaten by the cows – with the result that all the milk tasted of onions. To me, this did not matter all that much, but many of the chaps would not drink a drop of milk for two or three weeks.

There was in our flight an airman named Thomas, whose mother in England had given him the advice that he should be very careful not to get too near the aeroplanes when they were started up, an excellent warning, because during World War I, there were many serious accidents when propellers were swung by hand. Thomas's mother could not be expected to know that we now had battery trucks. I well recall how a Barkston man named Allott, who joined the Royal Flying Corps, was struck on his head by a propeller that he was swinging, and he never fully recovered from his injuries.

An airframes rigger by the name of Thomas, a street bookmaker's clerk, went to morning roll call and immediately went for his breakfast (his usual practice), but was caught by Sergeant Lowe and for this got five days 'Jankers'.

One of the trainee pilots had also been in trouble. He had, whilst flying, dived low over a house, carried away its wireless aerial and dented the cowlings of one engine. His excuse was that he had collided with a Swainson's Hawk. Unfortunately for him, the presence of wire and insulators wrapped about the engine belied his tale.

Our 'D' flight had also been in trouble again, for at the 7.00 a.m. parade we were told by Flight Sergeant Smith that the previous day he had found three men asleep on their beds during the afternoon. He warned us that serious action would be taken if we did not give more co-operation and do a bit more work.

The flying side were not without their own problems, because Wing Commander Armour had to fail a pupil who had told him that he had neither confidence in himself nor in the two-motored Anson planes. I dare say that he felt a bit frustrated, or was fed up with the rather rough treatment that some of the instructors gave to the pupil pilots. Not infrequently, whilst flying myself, I heard the instructor carrying on alarmingly, calling the trainee such names as 'idiot' over the simplest of mistakes. In many ways it was a rough war.

At first we had no barber on the camp. One of the things that was done was to find an old chap in the town who came up and cut our hair for us. He had the use of an unused room in one of the hangars, where the only seat was a well-worn carpenter's trestle. We were allowed to get our hair cut during working hours, and I think that we paid about 10 cents to the barber. Usually this old chap was talkative – according to him he had cut the hair of many Native Americans. He said that they all had black hair, as straight as a reed, and never had he seen a bald Native American. One of his advices to us was never to use the showers because much of the water was alkaline, and that soon thinned down a thick head of hair. He had seen Norwegian settlers come to Canada with lovely heads of golden hair, but the water soon finished that off. I think that the old chap was right about this, because I know that it thinned out what little hair I had on the top of my own head.

By midsummer the station routine had, in my opinion, settled down quite nicely. Discipline had been tightened up considerably. We all had to march to and from work. As a general rule we erks were not untidy at work, but sometimes the flight sergeant would hold us all up outside the hangar while somebody went back to clear up bits of old rag or patches of oil on the hangar floor.

I was classified as a leading aircraftsman and later passed the test for promotion to a fitter II (Engines) with a small increase in pay. There were ample opportunities to fly when planes that we had repaired were under test conditions and we got the RCAF flying allowance payment, which was better than the RAF rate.

Flying went on all day and sometimes for much of the night. Generally one could say that we mechanics worked quite hard and gave a reasonably good performance, in spite of one or two new regulations about discipline. There were odd times when we had to wait a short time for spare parts from a central store in Winnipeg. On one occasion we had to send to Winnipeg for some special bolts that secured the engines to the airframe. They arrived late one afternoon and were put aside until the morning. When we went to work next day, it was found that somebody had stolen them. There were times when we had to search the scrap heap to see whether we could find serviceable fittings. Most of the chaps worked well, although it has to be admitted that, as in all walks of life, there were some who prided themselves on dodging the column.

5

Plane Crashes and an Overturned Tractor

Accidents seldom happen singly – we had two on 29 July 1942.

For some unknown reason Anson 8528, whilst taking off on the east facing runway and about fifty feet in the air, suddenly veered to the left, lost height as it turned in a semicircle, and crashed slap bang into the open doors of No.4 hangar. Actually I saw it all happen from where I stood about 50 yards away. I was among the dozen or so chaps who rushed into the hangar. When I heard an airman say that one member of the crew had one eyeball hanging down his cheek, this was too much for me, for I never liked the sight of blood. I never knew the name of the pupil, who was so seriously injured that he died during the morning in the station hospital. An instructor in the plane was Pilot Officer Moon. He too was badly injured and I think that he also died the same day. As always in the service, no precise details of the cause of the accident were made known.

Within an hour the news came round that an instructor had taken Instrument Repairer Bill Cant with him in a Tiger Moth aircraft for a joyride. Not far outside the airfield boundary something had gone wrong, the machine crash-landed, caught fire and both men were killed. Bill Cant was a pleasant young chap who lived in the next barrack room to mine and he was well liked all round. One of his room mates wrote to his parents in England telling them what had happened. They soon wrote back asking for more details of the mishap. I rather think that they felt perhaps the RAF authorities had not told them the whole truth.

A few days afterwards, during night flying, a pupil fell into the trees that lined the river valley bordering the airfield's western boundary. Fortunately, he suffered minor injuries only.

One morning in October there was a mishap with a motor tractor. A corporal named Kennedy, perched high on the seat of this tractor, came racing along a fairly high speed towards No.4 hangar, turned sharply, went too close to Anson 8558 that had just been pushed out of the hangar and for some reason hit the main plane of this aircraft. The tractor turned on its side and Kennedy was thrown off it onto the ground. The tractor engine continued to run and somehow or other the tractor managed to right itself, turned a half circle and headed back to the aircraft. Kennedy had just enough time to jump onto 8558's tail plane before the tractor hit the plane's fuselage and swung the plane round and round like a roundabout. Kennedy fell off the tail plane, narrowly avoiding being run over. About half a dozen chaps looked on, quite helpless to do anything and just waiting for a big pile-up. I ran to get the fire brigade. When I got back a squadron leader had chased the tractor, jumped on it and stopped it. The whole episode seemed funny enough – it was like watching cowboys riding heifers in a wild west display.

6

Farming and General

Agricultural farming was the chief activity for hundreds of miles around Estevan. Barley, wheat and oats were the principal crops. An alternative was to grow, for green feed for animals, a green-leafed crop of a yellow-flowered plant called alfalfa that grew to a height of about four feet. Some maize was also grown, but we were a little too far north for this crop to ripen, so it, too, had to be used as a green feed for farm animals. Farmers did not plough their land in autumn as is the custom with British farmers. When I asked a farmer why this was so he said that by leaving the stubble it was a means of holding the winter snow from blowing straight across the fields and ending up in ditches or hedges. At the spring thaw it was most important to have the moisture scattered across the whole of each field where it would provide the germination of the seed corn and get it off to a good start. The moisture content of the soil was a summer worry for all farmers; it was also a feature of the newspapers. One saving grace was the frequent summer thunderstorms and much lightning that brought nitrogen-rich rain which, within an hour or so, put a healthy dark green colour on to the standing crops.

When the farmers seeded their crops they did not use deep ploughs. Instead, they usually went over the ground with a shallow tined cultivator before drilling the seed into the old stubble. Quite close to the airfield I saw a field that was treated in this fashion. The young wheat sprouted up through the stubble, which was carpeted with a mass of dwarf wild roses in full pink blossom.

Wheat could be seriously damaged by a pest called sawfly.

This creature thrived in loose soil before laying its eggs in the wheat straw. When the grubs hatched out, they ate holes in the wheat straw, causing it to fall and ruin the crop. In May there was an article in *The Winnipeg Tribune* warning the farming community that the sawfly grubs were hatching out. The same newspaper also reported that the Bishop of the Arctic had just married a headmistress. His diocese is a cold one of 2,500,000 square miles. The Inuit of the north call their Bishop *In-Nook-Tah-Kant*, which means 'one of the family of Inuit'.

August and September were the busy months for the farmers, when it was all go for everyone in that big gathering of people of many nationalities – English, French, German, Russian, in fact, somebody from almost every European country. On the whole it seemed as though they had settled in together very well, sharing their implements and animals in a workable community spirit. A man once told me that their method was to make gangs that one day threshed for one man and then moved on to do another man's work. He said that he felt English settlers were least willing to accept these arrangements, as they had little time for this community work method.

South Saskatchewan's farming land was not, generally speaking, very fertile. Official figures showed that between 1926 and 1932 there had been an exodus of no fewer than 50,000 people from south to north Saskatchewan.

If one looked at the collection of ancient and often battered old cars in which many of these farmers motored into town, one had a reliable yardstick of the degree of prosperity of this farming community, or lack of it. The whole area was one of cars on their last few years of life.

Although this happened just over the border in the USA to some extent, the old-car complex was not so marked. One day when I was hitch-hiking in North Dakota, I was given a lift by an old lady of about 80 who had a Model T Ford. When we stopped at a garage to get some petrol, gas they called it, she wanted to check the oil level in the gearbox. To do this she had to kneel down on the ground holding a three foot metal rod and reach the two test taps under the gearbox.

Before the coming of the white man there were huge flocks of wild pigeon that lived on the western prairies, but, as in the case of the wild buffalo, they were annihilated completely. The buffalo did not provide beef of very high quality, but what finished them off was shooting them for their tongues only. These titbits were sent east to markets in railway wagons. Later on I was shown areas where the first farming settlers found their lands littered with the skeletons of buffalo. The only traces now of these wild animals are the skulls and horns that are nailed over the doors of some farm barns.

The wild duck managed to survive, and, helped by preservation measures, the population of them increased from 25,000,000 in 1925, to 60,000,000 in 1939.

7

Visits to the USA

During June 1942 the weather turned dry and hot. It seemed to me that as the USA border was so near and inviting, it was time that I made a few excursions into this interesting country. My first real attempt was to go to Noonan, a largish village of around 200 people, about four miles over the border. Canada and the USA were separated by a plain wire fence. The two countries each had their own customs posts; both were made up of wooden buildings, although the USA buildings were more impressive affairs. All that was required of me was to give my name and address and destination. Once over the line I formed the opinion that the soil looked better than in Canada and that the crops, too, were somewhat better. I walked towards Noonan and very soon came to a single line railway belonging to the Great Northern Railway of America. Beside this railway stood two white-painted elevators quite 50 feet high. A farmer was carting loose grain to this elevator in a horse-drawn wagon. In contrast to our British practice of putting grain into sacks, these farmers of the prairies loaded it into open wagons that were tipped into the bins of these elevators, where their contents were taken to the top of them on conveyor belts. All over the prairies one saw these railside elevators, for they form one of the chief features of the countryside.

The elevator foreman came up to me and we got into conversation. He offered me, a very light smoker, a cigar. Part of the conversation was how to win the war, although neither of us knew a deal about the right way to do so. This man said that his father was Irish and that his wife had been born in Alsace.

Standing a little way off, beside two derelict steam engines, there was a group of men. I went over to them and saw that they were drinking whisky from a bottle. When I declined a drink offered to me, they all looked surprised and one of them said that he had never before met a non-drinking Englishman. However, they then took some wine from the back of a car and I did drink some of that.

The two old traction engines were of American construction and were much lighter in weight than our British traction engines. They had been used for ploughing and threshing; one had two cylinders and the other had only one cylinder bolted onto the side of its boiler. Both engines had round water tanks stuck on their front and rear ends. They were awaiting rail transport to go away for scrap. One has to remember that the internal combustion-engined tractor ousted the steam engines from the farms of America much earlier than in Britain.

As the evening was coming on, I turned west towards Crosby, but I had not gone far before a thrush-sized bird with a red breast that the local people called a robin flew up from the roadside grass and objected to my presence by circling my head and making plunges at my face, so close that its wing tips almost touched my cheeks. Doubtless it had a nest nearby. As I walked on I came past several large ponds, or prairie sloughs, each of which had a small population of wild duck.

I soon became aware that a large, very dark bank of clouds was building up in front of me to the west. Flashes of forked lightning were coming from this storm and there was the distinct roll of thunder. Fortunately, I was passing a roadside farm as the first drops of rain fell, so I ran into the large barn for shelter. Almost immediately the rain and hail fell and there was a violent wind. Hailstones as big as large marbles bounced as they bombarded the ground. Inside the barn, I found that the farmer and his family were Swedish. The farmer, his father, wife and daughter were in the barn milking their 12 cows. When the storm abated a little, I was asked to go into the farmhouse, which had clean white paint everywhere and was spotlessly clean. The whole family was worried that the great hail might spoil their crops, but fortunately this did not happen. They told me of occasions when the hail was so fierce as to knock dents into the roofs of their cars, cattle could be killed, or they could be knocked senseless and take a couple of days to recover. I was invited to have supper with them – we had hot tomato soup, with biscuit, butter and jam, followed by stewed plums and black coffee. I told these kind people that I would not try to get any further on the road that night, so the farmer took me in his car back to Noonan, where I went into the Travellers' Hotel for the night.

I never knew the name of these Swedish people who had been so kind to me. Let me say that they were, on the whole, the kind of helpful people whom I met all over the USA and Canadian prairies.

All that night, as I lay in my hotel bed, I heard the thunder and saw the lightning of the storm. In the morning I noticed that the water in the hotel was the colour of milk. According to the Norwegian landlord, it was town water pumped from 300 feet down in the ground and although it also had an unpleasant taste, it was good drinking water. I found that it did not upset me.

In this hotel I met a Railway station agent, station master, who told me that the Great Northern Railway of the USA now had huge oil-fired steam locomotives that could handle very long freight trains over the 1,000 miles from Seattle to St. Paul.

Life in the RAF meant that one never knew how long one would be in one place; sudden postings elsewhere were bound to come along. I found that it was wise to have a good look around wherever one happened to be at the moment. So, having looked at a map of the USA, I saw that the Missouri River, one of the large rivers of America, was only about a 100 miles south as it passed through Williston. I decided to make a trip to it on my next 48 hour weekend leave.

There were thunderstorms hanging about as I booked out at the guardroom. I walked about ten miles to Noonan and it was a very slow hitch-hike to Crosby. I did not get there until after 6.00 p.m. Having decided that it was too late in the day to go further, I booked a room at the Allen Hotel. About 7.00 p.m. the landlady came up to my room, saying that she had heard me say that I was making for Williston. A man named Mr Russell, who was a district inspector for some banks and insurance companies had come into the hotel, would be taking a drink before setting out to Williston in his chauffeur-driven car in about ten minutes and he would take me there. The Latvian landlady said that she would reserve the room that I had booked for the following evening. It did not matter how late I was, all I had to do was to come in through the unlocked hotel door and go up to my room. All this seemed too good to be true and I accepted the arrangement immediately.

Mr Russell was a largish late middle-aged man wearing a wide-brimmed hat. His 42 horsepower Buick car was a fine big model and in a few minutes we were off to a flying start with me in the back seat. The chauffeur was named Edwin Larsen, a Norwegian. He wore a floppy sort of hat, decorated with several silver-coloured badges. Mr Russell was a typical American, a bit brusque in his manner, who called me 'Kid', or said, 'Oh hell, no,' in his replies. He questioned me closely, wanting to know my nationality, where I had come from and what I was doing in the States. He said that his father had at one time kept the saloon, pub, at a place called Dog Dyke near Boston in Lincolnshire. I told him that I knew the place and, in fact, had come from Coningsby airfield very close to it. I had the feeling that both of them thought that I was a bit of a line shooter. Mr Russell turned around and asked me why I was going to Williston.

When I said that I was wanting to see the Missouri river, he turned to his chauffeur and said, 'Well, did you hear that?' To me he said, 'You are the first person that I have ever met who wanted to see that.'

'Why not,' I said, 'Isn't it one of the great rivers of America?'

Mr Russell then said, 'Where are you staying in Williston?' and when I said that I hoped to get into the Great Northern Hotel, he replied, 'We, too, are going there; you must join us at supper and you shall have some Missouri catfish, for they are regarded as a great delicacy here.'

We all had supper together and I found that the catfish were excellent eating.

As we had sped along in the car I had noticed that all the road was paved with gravel. The fields were full of almost ripe wheat, fairly well littered with yellow sunflowers that were just weeds, not quite as high as the wheat.

My room at the hotel was a very comfortable one, with hot water and a shower – also it had a phone. The first thing I did in the morning was to walk into the town and buy a small Bantam camera for four American dollars. The girl in the shop gave me a present of a new film. Mr Russell devoted the morning to business calls, so, along with the chauffeur, I went to have a look at the railway station.

A large diesel-electric locomotive was shunting at the head of a 150 wagon train, and it looked so far away that it looked little more than a mere dot. Some of the wagons, cars they called them, had a load capacity of 100,000 pounds.

An eastbound passenger train came in whilst we were at the station. The locomotive was a large oil-fired steam engine, and the conductor came up to us and invited us to step up into the cab of the 2-8-4 machine. The inside of its cab was somewhat dirty, but it was full of various pipes and levers. We were told by the engine driver that he and his mate were finishing their turn of duty, but we could ride with them to the loco depot about half a mile away. We did so, and while looking around the outside of the engine I noticed that there were air holes towards the bottom of the firebox. These holes passed right through the water spaces and, in fact, you could see the fire inside the firebox. Never before had I seen anything like that and I could only assume that outside ventilation like that was a feature of assistance to good combustion in an oil-burning locomotive. The driver of the engine asked me if I were a Scotsman, because he was sure that I spoke like one.

Edwin Larsen and I then returned to the hotel, where Mr Russell then very kindly treated me to lunch. All through the meal, Mr Russell talked about American game animals and birds in a very knowledgeable way. I found that he was great company. After lunch he set off again, this time to Montana where he had further business. I thanked him for his great kindness in entertaining me.

Early in the afternoon I set off to see the Missouri River; there was a bridge that crossed it north to south and I had about five miles to walk. I very soon noticed that the road was littered with the dead bodies of snakes that had been killed by passing motors. These reptiles were rounded in shape, greenish in colour, and they did not look poisonous. At this point the river turned towards the road and through a hedge I could see that there was a clump of willow trees standing in marshy ground, so it seemed obvious to me that the snakes were either going to a wettish place, or going towards the drier ground of a farmer's field.

I had a lift in a farmer's truck for about four miles to the huge bridge that crossed the river. At the entrance to this steel girder bridge there was a road sign that read, 'To the Badlands'. I crossed the river to the south. The actual width of the stream was about 320 yards of yellowish water, but it had a flood plain of quite a mile, bounded by 10 to 15 feet high retaining banks.

It so happened that an official of the river board was taking one of the routine checks, so we had quite a long chat. He was measuring the rate of flow of the water, by lowering a spinner into the water, listening at the end of the cable and counting the number of times the vane of the spinner rotated, which gave him the speed of the water. That afternoon it was 2 m.p.h. He told me that there were no rattlesnakes north of the river, but plenty on the other side.

I was much impressed by this great river, even if it was a tributary to the mighty Mississippi and not navigable at that point. I was told that the discoloration of the water was due to the silt-laden Yellowstone River that joined the Missouri about 20 miles upstream. This prompted me to have a shot at getting to this confluence and I set off west straight away. However, rides were not forthcoming, and I walked a long way.

The GNR Railway followed the road about a hundred yards on my left-hand side and I noticed that there was quite a small cloud of smoke in the distance. There was a little side road that led under a bridge carrying the railway, so, thinking to take a photograph of the train, I turned into this side road. As I did so, I noticed that two men sitting on a two-horse cart were approaching from the west. These men, to my surprise, turned into the lane and caught me up, stopped and asked me who I was and what I was doing. I told them that I was an RAF man from Canada and that all I was doing was intending to take a photograph of the approaching freight train. This satisfied them and they told me that they thought I was one of those Germans who was about to blow up the bridge and the train with it. Having satisfied themselves that I was not a German saboteur, the two young chaps became quite talkative. I brought up my usual subject about snakes in the area. To this, one of them said that there were bull snakes in the area but they were not poisonous.

However, he continued, an outstretched arm pointing to some hills about five or six miles to the north west, 'In those hills over there the soil is alkaline and there are poisonous snakes called blue racers, which are very long and thin, and so fast that a racehorse cannot keep up with them. I have only seen one of these snakes, and it shot in front of me in a field at great speed.'

As it was now about 4.00 p.m. I decided to give up my intention of going to the Yellowstone River, so I went back to Williston and had my tea in a little cafe before setting out on the road to the north.

Just outside the town there was a cobbler's shop that was still open. My shoes were well worn down after so much walking on the roads, so I went in and had a few nails put in the soles. Both the cobbler and his neighbour seemed to think they were lucky to meet an English soldier. All men in uniform were soldiers to the Americans. They wanted to hear all about the German air raids on Britain, as well as what I thought about Churchill and Roosevelt as leaders. It was 7.00 p.m. before I got away and I soon found that I could get hardly any rides towards Crosby.

It turned out that I had made a big mistake in delaying my departure. What lifts I got, between long walks, were from farmers who were going home to their farms. It began to get dark and a small owl circled my head closely two or three times. The stars came out and the Milky Way shone across the sky. What cars there were on the road seemed to be going the wrong way. Then I heard the thunder of a herd of horses running wild on the open prairie, but fortunately they passed without coming over the road. I never came to any dwelling or side road of any consequence. At 1.00 a.m. the light of an approaching car appeared. I stopped it in order to ask if there was any chance of a place where I might stay, only to be told that there was nothing at all like that and off it went on its way. The car stopped when it had gone about a hundred yards and came back to me. There was a young man driving it, with two teenage girls. They told me that they felt that I was in a bit of a fix and, although they had been to a dance in Crosby, they would go back there.

At the hotel, I found that the door was open, as promised by the landlady. Although I had little money on me, I gave the young chap an American dollar for his kindness After breakfast in the morning I hitched back to the frontier and Estevan.

8

Progress of the War

Although we were away from the active theatres of the war, the chaps in general followed its progress by listening to the radio news bulletins, both Canadian and those of the USA. There was a general feeling of disappointment when, in June, we heard that Rommel's troops were already 60 miles into Egypt. At the same time we were told that on one of Britain's night raids into Germany we had lost no fewer than 50 bomber planes. A month later, while I was reading in the Hostess Club in Estevan, I heard that the Germans had taken Matruh in Egypt.

When the USA came into the war in 1942 many people expected early successes, but this did not come about until much later. A Canadian newspaper reported that the All India Congress had some leanings towards negotiating with Japan. In October the Americans admitted that the Japanese had landed troops on the Solomon Islands, whilst Japan at the same time claimed that they had sunk two USA battleships and four USA aircraft carriers. Personally, I held the view that Churchill would know what, in good time, he would do. One bit of more heartening news was the report that a prominent Japanese statesman had said that Japan, in attacking the USA, had awakened a sleeping giant of great danger to Japan. This view was eventually proved right.

Several airmen had been in trouble. Nolan, McArdell and Hemmingway had been put under arrest following a brawl in Minot, USA.

It seems that one of them asked the time of an American who replied, 'I'm not telling you; it's a damned shame that our boys are fighting for you overseas, whilst all you English airmen do is to come here and play about with our women.'

As a result of this affair, all leave to the USA had been stopped. There was little doubt that this view was held by many Americans and Canadians. I suppose that something similar has arisen in all past wars.

Another thing that the Americans specially had against Britain was the view that our class system in Britain would have to go after the war. Several Americans who I met held this opinion and it was of little use for me to say that only a very few Britishers now bowed, or raised their hat to the squire, for so many Americans were firmly of the opinion that they did. They felt that we still lived in a feudal age.

However, it did seem that, at long last, we had a put a stop to the headlong advances of the German armies in Europe. In the event it was proved that they had bitten off more than they could control.

9

No.38 SFTS Gets into its Stride

Steadily, but surely, the progress at Estevan went ahead, more flying was done and quite a few improvements were made about meals, working conditions and camp entertainment.

We mechanics had got used to the mechanisms of the Jacobs engines, and we had no real difficulties with them. One very hot day, after working on an engine on Anson 8430, I had to go up with a pilot on a proving flight. Both engines ran very smoothly at 2,100 r.p.m. When at about 6,000 feet, the pilot put the plane into a steep dive and then lifted it up until it fell. The falling sensation was never to my liking and I clutched the frames of the co-pilot's seat, whilst my stomach turned over. I never liked those stall tests.

So far as the Jacobs engines were concerned, we fitters found them easier to service than our British engines. When an engine had to be retimed for the correct sparking point our British engines' maintenance manuals stipulated that we must use a lamp and battery box. Not so the American manuals, which just said, 'Tear a piece of cellophane from your cigarette box, place it between the ignition points, turn the propeller, and as soon as you can withdraw the cellophane, that is the timing point which must register with the engine timing point'. We did not have any really big troubles with these engines, but the metal lugs that secured the engines to the aircraft frame did have a habit of breaking and needed renewal quite a bit. One big fault was that the fractures that occurred on their crank cases meant a complete engine change, but for this the engines had to be sent to a main servicing depot in Winnipeg.

One day Anson 8582 came home from Bear Lake in the north

with the starboard engine's propeller almost completely broken off; only a few splinters remained on the hub. Most people thought that the pilot had done well to get home on one engine. Shortly afterwards we were told to pay special attention to the pressure that we put on the propeller securing bolts of all planes. Special spanners fitted with pressure gauges were supplied to us. Warrant Officer Green gave us a lecture on the subject. I never forgot the words with which he finished his talk.

'What you do is your affair. I'm telling you what you must say if a visiting group captain asks you.'

Another mishap instance occurred when Anson 8581 came in with a large brownish grey plumaged bird all tangled up in one engine. There were also several large dents in the engine cowling, as well as a broken spark plug lead. When the remains of the bird were removed from the engine fittings, they were given to a stray kitten that happened to be around and obviously very hungry. I think that it was common practice among the aircrews to dive at these hawks, for the sheer devilment of it, and something else to do.

For some time I looked after Anson 8430. Fortunately it showed up quite well for flying hours. One day, however, a pupil who was training his moustache to curl up around his upper lip to make himself look like a real wartime pilot, came into the crewroom saying that the starboard engine had stopped on the runway and he could not get it started again. I went with him and set the slow running control at its mid position, switched on to the battery, and the engine started immediately. In order to assure the pilot that the engine was OK, I went up with him for another circuit, although it was against orders for ordinary airmen to fly with a pupil without another officer on board. We landed during a rainstorm and, as he bounced heavily on the runway with a heavy bump, I did not think that this pupil was the best of the trainee pilots.

Odd and perhaps not very important things used to happen. Corporal Napper came into the barrack block one night after being out drinking, urinated in his overboot and left a stream running all over the floor.

One day, as I was leaving the airmen's mess with a cup of tea in one hand, the station Warrant Officer shouted after me saying, 'Throw it away.'

When I did so he just laughed. It was of course forbidden to take either food or drink away from the mess. Although he did ask for my name, I never heard any more about this minor incident.

One day Corporal Forstead came to me to ask whether I was prepared to volunteer for retraining as an air-gunner and, if not, would I give my reasons. I declined, for it did seem to me that the present aircraft losses were very high, with a consequent equal loss of air-gunners. Furthermore, my eyesight was not all that wonderful, neither had I the nerve for an air-gunner's duties.

At work there was usually plenty to do, although at times things were easy. There were times when some chaps had to be on duty at 5.00 a.m. until midday; they had to come on again at 5.30 p.m. and work at bringing the planes into the hangars, followed by having to do a spell of daily inspections in readiness for the next morning's flying.

One day, whilst hitch-hiking in the USA, I came up with three boys who were playing at lassoing next to a big red barn by the roadside. When one of these boys noticed the small shoulder wings on my tunic, he promptly asked me where I had left my plane, thinking that the small insignia that all airmen wore on their shoulder meant that I was a pilot. Some months later, when a fellow mechanic named Rickard and I were in Montana and close to a recruiting centre of the US army, every recruit we met in the town promptly saluted us, until we got so tired of this that we went back into our hotel for the rest of the evening. These chaps too, saw the shoulder wings and assumed that they indicated that we were pilot officers. Our RAF pilots wore much larger wings on their left breasts.

At Estevan we had the regular Sunday morning church parades, although Sunday was an ordinary working day and I did not attend too regularly. I well remember how a big Scottish parson who was visiting Canadian air stations told us in a big booming but pleasant voice that he hoped the war would soon be over and that once more we could be able to take the road to the Western Isles.

In an attempt to improve our national pride, a flag hoisting ceremony was held every day at 8.00 a.m. This meant detailing a small party of men, an NCO and an officer. Sometimes they added about ten minutes' drill. In addition to such stunts, there were many improvements in our working and general conditions. the food was improved and we had nightly cinema shows.

One evening while Frank Dowell and I were walking around Estevan, we chanced to go into the town cemetery. We found that the graves of several men who had been killed while flying had been very roughly filled in. Two empty graves were waiting for the next unfortunates. It was to be remembered that in Canada the frozen ground is too hard for any graves to be dug in winter.

The times of the opening of the dining room were altered from time to time. Once it closed at 7.30 a.m. when there had often built up a small queue of men waiting to get inside. On one such occasion a locked out airman came back with a note signed by a corporal saying that the man had been on duty at 5.30 a.m. This of course was a lie, but it was not until the corporal came back and argued with the cookhouse staff that the airman was admitted for his breakfast.

10

A Wet Saturday Afternoon

It was seldom that we had a straightforward rainy day on the prairies, for most of the rain came from the frequent thunderstorms. There was, about ten miles east of us, a place called Roche Percée, after some unusually split rocks that were there. I decided that I would go there myself and that I would walk over the rough prairie grasslands for a change from hitch-hiking. One Saturday afternoon I set off. The first thing that I came across was a dark hole in a low hillside that turned out to be the entrance to a soft coal mine, now abandoned – perhaps by the local farmer. About four miles further on, it came on to rain as I was passing a tiny sort of smallholding bordering on the Souris River. There happened to be an abandoned steam traction engine in the far corner of this bit of land, as it had once been used to pump water out of the river, probably for irrigation purposes. The smoke box of this old engine was wide open and the weather had washed away all the soot from its sides. I decided that I would jump into the smoke box for shelter from the increasing rain. It must have been an hour or so before I heard a woman's voice calling some cows across the river. I called out to her and explained who I was and that I wanted to know if there was a bridge across the river not too far away. She said that it was her house that could be seen among some tall poplar trees. Her French parents lived in a tiny house on the plot where I stood and that if I walked back a few hundred yards there was a wooden bridge across the river. I should come over to her side, and to her house, where she and her husband lived. I did so while the rain continued to fall heavily.

These people laid some supper consisting of coffee and ham sandwiches. They explained that they were going by car to some place in the opposite direction to Estevan for some Saturday night shopping, but they would take me to the Dominion Electricity generating station which was in the Estevan direction. The husband's name was Monsella, but that was all I ever knew of these kind folks. When we got to the power station I was handed over to the shift foreman who was named Newton. He was dressed in a clean boiler suit and one of his jobs was to stoke the boilers. He said that I was very welcome to stay the night with him and his wife. He could see that I was drenched through from being out in the rain and insisted that I took off my uniform and put it on the hot boiler pipes. He gave me a clean boiler suit which I put on while my uniform got dry. At 10.00 p.m. Mr Newton's shift finished and we went into his house where I was introduced to his wife. She made supper for us – we had toast and coffee.

The Newtons gave me a small but very snug little bedroom, with a window that gave a look out over their ten acre garden. When I went to bed I could hear the gently rustling of the leaves on some poplar trees. In the morning I had a look around the garden; I was shown their lily pond and a fountain. The pond made a home for about 30 large green frogs. These creatures were quite tame; they sat all around the pond and as one walked towards them they merely jumped obligingly into the water until one had passed, when they promptly jumped out again onto the lawn grass.

I was asked to stay for lunch and was promised that first thing afterwards the Newtons would run me over to the Estevan airfield in their car. How wonderfully well treated I was by these very kind folks.

11

A Look at the Rocky Mountains

Frank Dowell and I both wanted to see the Rocky Mountains, so we palled up and went to see them in late September 1942. We took our 14 days annual leave, with a 48 hours weekend leave at the beginning. Sergeant Hilliard let me finish at noon on the Friday, so I nipped off, had a quick lunch in the dining room, before catching a bus down to Estevan, where I got the railway tickets to a town called Lethbridge. I think that we had railway warrants that entitled us to a cheap rate, but I am not now sure about this. Frank was kept back at work for some reason, but he did manage to be down at the station for us to catch the 3.10 p.m. westbound train. The Rockies were about 500 miles west of us, so we travelled all that day and night getting to Lethbridge. I remember that a Canadian sailor in the train told me that the German battleship *Bismark* was propelled by diesel engines.

As the train approached Lethbridge, dawn was breaking and I had my first sight of the mountains. They looked like a long line of a bronze-coloured barrier, with the first snow on the tops of the higher peaks. What a change it was for me to see some high ground after a year on pretty flat prairie country. In fact, it gave me quite a sudden feeling of exhilaration. These mountains were an unforgettable sight.

Our plan was to start in the south of our trip and gradually work upwards, finishing up around Banff and the Kicking Horse Pass. We stayed the first day in Lethbridge, before setting off the next day westwards. The mountains were still 50 miles away. The countryside was, from the start, rather brown and featureless and of an arid nature.

After walking for a couple of miles we were picked up by a very pleasant man from Calgary. He took us to a little place called McLeod, where he insisted upon entertaining us to lunch in a cafe. At table he talked about the railway builders around Medicine Hat and how they tied harmless bull snakes around the workmen's tents in order to keep rattlesnakes away. It was a lovely day of Indian Summer weather, with a cloudless sky, and the first few autumn colours had begun to brighten up the countryside. From McLeod, a Scotsman took us to a place called Cowley, where we went into a beer parlor in which there was a drunken old Belgian who had just drawn his pension. He would treat us to a drink and, indeed, that was how everybody seemed to think that they owed us something.

Then we were taken in a farm motor truck through very pretty country, along a road that ran through the foothills of the mountains, with their rugged peaks capped with a dusty coating of snow. These mountains formed a great western wall to the prairies and, indeed, they were the west wall of North America. The driver of the truck told us that we were approaching the site known as Frank's Slide where, in 1903, at 5.00 a.m. on a Sunday morning 50,000,000 tons of rock of the mountainside broke away and fell on the village of Frank below with its 66 folks, and buried them for ever. We were also told that there were extensive coal mines in the same mountain – some of the seams were as much as 30 feet thick. At the time of this great mishap there were a number of miners in the mine working, but fortunately the rock fall left sufficient gaps for the miners to escape. The road upon which we had travelled lay over the great tumble of fallen rocks. We went on to Coleman, where we put up in the Grand Union Hotel, a clean place with a good restaurant next door.

At Coleman there was a big metal mining and smelting industry. A large coke-making kiln belched out smoke and flames all night long. Somebody pointed out to us the distant Crow's Nest Mountain, with a smoke mist creeping up its summit at 10,000 feet. In past times, a watchman was posted on the slope of this mountain, as a lookout man for seeing the approach of bands of hostile Native Americans.

Next morning we were given a ride by a Scotsman who took us

to Fernie, about 30 miles away. We had lunch there. Whilst we were eating, a Canadian Reserve soldier, rather under the influence of drink, came up to us and told us that a local man named Bert Sadler always entertained airmen in his house, where we should sleep in lovely silk and satin beds with gladiolas spreading over them. How drink seems to make poets out of some men! We went on our journey north. As we went along the road a colourful front garden caught our eyes. A lady came out of the house to tell us that the flowers were called Golden Glow. She was Czech and her husband was a Slav. She then walked a mile with us and we exchanged addresses, promising to write at Christmas, but I do not think that we, nor she, did so.

Another car soon picked us up and we sped over the route of a pulled up railway track to Elks where an elderly lady told us to keep away from the girls. We next walked about two or three miles before being picked up and taken to Cranbrook, where we put up at the Hotel Byng. Next morning we set off again, with the mountains quite close on our left-hand side. What a glorious change it was from the almost endless spread of the flat prairies of Estevan.

Our ride next day was given by a new type of driver who happened to be a mine official returning from a hunting trip in the mountains. He told us that in the back of his car he had a modern set of hunting equipment in the form of bows and arrows, by which he claimed that he could kill big game more surely than by a rifle. The arrows were three feet long and tipped with barbs. He had seen a moose shot through the chest and the arrowhead had come out of the hind quarters.

All the way along the roads through the foothills, people told us that the mountains were full of bears.

Kimberley was a town of some 5,000 people; there was also the largest lead and zinc mine in the world. Whilst we were staying there in the Globe Hotel, somebody told us that we ought to see the Concentration Plant and, without any more fuss, somebody phoned up the plant and obtained permission for Frank and me to visit the place first thing next morning. We set off in good time and walked to the works, where we were shown huge grinding mills that ground the heavy black rock into powder.

Chemicals then floated off the lead and then the zinc. Finally, big ridged tables collected, or rather, floated off the ore. The remaining tin, silver, sulphuric acid, antimony, iron and a few other metals, were sorted out in the same way. All the metals were refined at Trail.

There were some maple trees standing outside the work's entrance and they were the first maple trees that I had seen in Canada, although they were not the sugar maples of Ontario. We came away with an invitation to call again in the morning to see the mine inside the mountain. During the evening we went into a beer parlor that had a separate partition for women. In Saskatchewan women were not allowed to go up to the bar in beer parlors. Two big men began a fight in which one of them got two badly cut eyes. A lady in the bar wiped off the blood. Shortly afterwards we got into conversation with a schoolmaster, who told us that 200 schools in British Columbia were closed for the want of teachers.

In the morning we got up at 7.30 a.m., and after breakfast we set off for the mine of the Mining Consolidation Company. It was approached by a long road that passed under a line of fine trees that looked fresh and slightly fringed with autumn colours, and the sun shone beautifully. When we arrived at the works we were dressed in mine gear comprising a suit of blue overalls, heavy boots and a bakelite helmet fitted with an electric lamp. A tall young engineer took charge of us. We all jumped onto a low electric locomotive that had a string of trucks coupled to it. Off we went at a fair speed for one and a half miles into the heart of the mountain. We found that the ore was taken from a very big and high cavity called a stoop. Just how the ore was let down into the bottom of this stoop without falling on the heads of the miners below, I never quite understood. A total of 10,000 tons of ore was taken out every day. During our two hours inside that stoop the air was rather damp and cool. All told, it was something well worth seeing.

As we left at the work's gate, the gateman pointed out a bush of wild Saskatoon berries, so I tried a few of them, but Frank would not risk this wild food. But somehow I got by. Incidentally, these blue/black berries had stones similar to our currants. I found them very tasteful indeed.

That afternoon, as we were walking along the road, a Canadian Pacific Railway official picked us up in his car and took us 46 miles to Canal Flats. He was the supervisor of a large sawmill that was making wooden doors for freight cars at the rate of one every five minutes. He suggested that we should travel north on a freight train that would leave shortly and he took us to this train on which the steam locomotive had two tenders, one of them for carrying water only. Next to this tender was an open freight car, or truck, that was loaded very lightly with new wooden sleepers for railway tracks and we were told to get up and ride in this truck. Neither the driver nor his fireman said a word of objection to what we did. However, shortly afterwards one of the train brakesmen came up and said that the ride would be a bit jerky, causing the sleepers to slide about and trap our legs.

'Get up on that second tender,' he said, 'and you'll be OK there.'

We did so without the enginemen saying a word, although I would have thought that they had more control of this vehicle than the brakesmen. Afterwards I learned from another man whilst we were on this trip that the brakesmen had wide powers in Canada and the USA. We soon set off and the sun shone gloriously as we puffed along among the autumn colours, passing lakes Colombia and Windermere. The water in the rivers and lakes was beautifully clear and in fact we could see quite large fish swimming about just under the surface. To say that this was a wonderful trip for us would be an understatement, for it remains with me as a run through an earthly paradise. When we arrived at a place called Invermere the locomotive was taken off and put in a siding, to be cared for by some employee or other until the enginemen arrived on duty again in the morning. We got down from the water tender and the driver said that we could find a night's accommodation at a little hotel just up the road, where he and his fireman would also be staying. When we went down to the evening meal, everyone sat down to a long table upon which there was a huge plate of golden boiled corn, or maize. I had one of these corns for my supper and it made excellent eating. During the meal, the girl who was waiting at table declined to give Frank another cup of tea, much to his annoyance. Although I was not sure, the reason may have been because of a rationing requirement. Next morning we once again took to the road, which passed through delightful countryside, and the autumn colours were almost overpowering. All along the roadsides there were wild raspberries to be picked and we saw a pair of white-tailed deer wandering through the pine and poplar trees. For part of the way we had a lift in a car to Radium Springs, where we arrived shortly after lunch time. We noticed a smart looking hotel called the Oliver Hotel that was run by a man called Casey Oliver, who asked us to come in saying that in the last war he had served as a officer in the army, and also in the North West Mounted Police.

'Now, gentlemen,' he said, 'I am sorry that we closed at the end of the season last weekend on Labour Day, but the bedrooms have not yet been stripped, so you can have a room. We cannot give you any food, but the restaurant up the road will be open.' We accepted this offer. He was a talkative man, and continued, 'As an old soldier, I will advise you both to take the rough times with the smooth – why not take an afternoon's nap on the settees in our upstairs lounge,'

As we chatted in the hall with this old soldier, his wife never said more than two words as she kept on knitting. Casey Oliver was very British and good company.

Radium Springs is popular with holidaymakers, mainly because there is a rock-bound swimming pool, where water at 115F pours from a hole in the rock. After dark, electric lights were switched on and Frank and I swam there on two evenings.

We ate at the Blakey restaurant. It had, in the dining room, a wild hop that had crept inside and had been trained to hang inside the west window with its great bunches of wild hops hanging down – all very pretty indeed.

The Sinclair stream ran down past both hotels and we noticed a path that ran under the hill. We saw a long carpet snake, mottled with brown patches, and it was watching us. When we came back it had disappeared.

At the Blakey's restaurant we found good company, mostly Americans, one of whom complained about the amount of her income tax. While we were there, Mr Blakey came in from hunting with a large Canada goose.

When we left Radium Springs at 10.00 next morning, we were given a fond farewell all round as we set off into the Kootenay Park. What a beautiful day it was as we walked alongside the tumbling waters of the Sinclair Creek. Small bushes that looked like gooseberries with their rusty yellow leaves gave an autumn look to the scene. Some of these bushes were also loaded with ripe black berries, a little bigger than our blackcurrants. Somebody afterwards told us that they were probably what we call pink flowering currants. Also growing by the roadside was another bush with yellowish leaves and some salmon-coloured berries that we were afterwards informed were salmon berries. The autumn colours of the wild rose bushes were a picture, with leaves of amber and the hips were far sweeter than our British ones. As we looked ahead, the high mountains stood out above the pine trees. There were few cars along this road, due to gas, petrol, rationing, and the fact that the holiday period was over. However, it did not matter so much to us because the walking was fine. We did, however, have to walk seven or eight miles without a lift, but eventually we sat down by the roadside, where we took out from our side bags some plum cake and apples to eat, almost opposite the cottage of a game warden. For drink, we hand-cupped stream water.

The next ten miles lifted us up over the 10,000 feet summit, but we did get a lot of luck being picked up by a chap called Ernie Oldfield, the driver of a timber lorry, who told us that he had emigrated from Leicester. For us this was a most fortunate encounter, for Ernie eventually took us right over the Kicking Horse Pass. That day he dropped us at a place called Rocky Mountains Cabins, saying that it would be a good place for us to stay that night. He himself would be spending the night a few miles further on and if we cared to walk to him next morning, he would take us on. His one stipulation was that we should be there by 8.00 a.m. This was agreed.

There were about a dozen modern cabins at Rocky Mountains House, owned by a man and his wife, for letting to holidaymakers. We settled for one night in a cabin called Mountain View, with a fully fitted interior. We had supper with the man and his wife, eating some delicious cut throat trout that they had caught that day. Whilst waiting for supper, I tried my hand at fishing, using a grasshopper as bait. Although I did hook one fish, it fell off. Whilst eating our supper, the house dog barked as a warning that a bear was about, so we all went out with electric hand torches, but all we saw was the reflected gleam from the bear's eyes as it passed over into the woods. Later on that evening, I did hang an apple on a piece of string over the outside window of our cabin, in order to see if a bear came to get it during the night. One end of the string was tied to a couple of small saucepans to make a noise, but nothing at all happened.

At 5.30 a.m. next morning we were up and lit the cabin fire and made breakfast. At about 7.00 a.m. we were out and on our way to go and find Ernie. It was a walk of several miles, but it was a lovely morning as the first animals were waking up and we could hear their calls. A furry little chipmunk with a bushy tail ran up a small fir tree and by its chatter made us aware that it did not care for our presence at all. From the valley on our right-hand side there came the bugle-like call of an elk. The world was just waking up.

We found Ernie busy loading up his lorry with some pitch pine planks, so we gave him a hand. Soon we were off, with the three of us sitting in the front of the otherwise open lorry cab. At the Vermilion River we stopped in order that Frank and I might see the deep river valley, with cascades of water boiling downwards from the mountain glaciers. The old truck pulled hard and slowly up the long climb of the 5,000 feet of the Vermilion Pass. The first 50 miles drive through the Kootenay and Banff National Parks passed through very pretty countryside, and we saw everything of it. At times it was a bit cold in the open cab, but we kept going and enjoying it all.

Ernie was good company, telling us all about himself and how he had tried most things: farming, road making, acting as a spare hand with packhorse survey parties and so on. He had also spent a period of work in the USA. All told, I formed the opinion that he had not made a fortune by emigrating to Canada.

At No.1 Highway we turned north, with the high Castle Mountain in front of us. Other rugged peaks also reared up on our left-hand side, all of them covered with snow and ice. At Lake Louise the Mountain View Hotel told us that they gave food only to residents. This meant that we had to be content with some biscuits and raisins that made a makeshift lunch.

One of the things that I really wanted to see was the Kicking Horse Pass and the spiral tunnels of the Canadian Pacific Railway.

As soon as Ernie heard about this, he immediately said, 'I will take you up to the Kicking Horse Pass and then across the mountain to Field on the other side. From there you could come back by the train and pass through the two spiral tunnels.'

We immediately agreed to this plan and after having climbed up the gravel strewn road with the heavily laden lorry, we came to the Kicking Horse Pass, where we stopped for a few minutes beside the Canadian Pacific Railway line. Going on, we came past the summit of the Great Divide at 5,330 feet elevation. A small rivulet runs along the top of the ridge and suddenly divides. One half of the stream turns west and runs down to take its waters into the Pacific Ocean, whilst the other turns east taking its waters across Canada and into the Atlantic Ocean. Although this may be one of the world's millions of watersheds, it has always held a special attraction for me.

We then started the long run down off the mountains into British Columbia, along most scenic countryside, until we stopped. Ernie then pointed out to us the railway station at Field, which was only about half a mile away up a side road.

'There's your place where you will be able to get a train back through the tunnels in the morning.'

We got down from the lorry and, with many heartfelt thanks for a lovely long ride, we said goodbye to Ernie. I often wonder whether he is still alive.

We had now been eight days on our holiday, and it was time to turn back. We booked a room at Field Station, in accommodation that had something to do with the YMCA. The beds were quite clean, but there was a lot of coal dust and small cinders about in the bedroom.

Field was the place where all eastbound trains had to be assisted by locomotives over the long climb inside the spiral tunnels inside the mountain. The assisting locomotives were huge machines. Passenger trains had an extra 2-8-4 locomotive in front, whilst the much heavier freight trains had two 2-10-4s in front and another one pushing at the rear. Late in the evening one of the big 2-10-4s came to stand outside our window. It had rows of electric lights hung along both sides of it. When it started off the exhaust beats from its chimney were thunderous. Much cinder and smoke was blown into our room.

Next morning we were up in good time, had a quick breakfast of coffee and cake in a YMCA canteen on the station and then bought tickets to Banff by the 7.05 a.m. train. Owing to the windows of our coach being misted over, we went to the next vehicle's corridor, but for some unknown reason one of the train's conductors, a black man, came along the corridor and turned us out very unceremoniously and firmly. It may have been because that coach was a sleeper vehicle and the man did not want people disturbed. We did, however, see a little of the scenery alongside the line. At one place near the summit there were several gravestones, doubtless the resting place of the bones of men who were killed during the construction of the line. We also saw several deer grazing off the frosted line-side grass.

At Banff we got off the train and walked two miles up a fairly steep climb to Lake Louise. This lake, nearly a mile and a half long, is one of the 'musts' for holiday makers. There are tall mountains on three sides of the water, which is a lovely deep blue colour. It is the amount of raw copper that is in the rocks of the mountains that gives it this colour. The huge Lake Louise Hotel is at the eastern end. It is owned by the Canadian Pacific Railway, but was now closed for the duration of the war. Victoria Mountain is across the distant western horizon. It is hung with glaciers – every five or fifteen minutes there came a low rumble like thunder and we were told that it was the tumble of snow and ice from the glaciers. Frank and I had a walk along the sides of the lake before going into the Deer Lodge Hotel for lunch. The sun shone so warmly that the blinds in the dining room had to be drawn.

Whilst we had been along the lake we had seen some rabbit-like creatures running about, so we enquired about the wildlife. The lady who ran the hotel told us that the whistling marmots had already started to hibernate.

'You see,' she said, 'the bears eat them, so, in self-preservation, they hibernate early.'

Probably it was a few odd ones of these marmots that we had seen. She went on to explain that these marmots were regarded by some people as survivors of the ice age During hibernation they do not breathe, but their blood continues to circulate.

Whilst walking back down the hill to Banff we came across a man scraping loose stones off the road. Before emigration he had been an employee of the London and North Western Railway, now he was still a jack of all trades. He told us that he had done many different jobs, both in the USA and in Canada. Here was another man who had not struck gold by emigrating. He also told us that at one time railway conductors of freight trains used to charge hitch-hiking hoboes, or tramps 50 cents per section, about 100 miles, to ride on freight trains. These conductors issued their own tickets and pocketed the money.

During the day Frank had been bothered with a bout of indigestion, so we were glad when a car picked us up. In this car were Mr and Mrs Bunny Falls, who were holidaying and just having a ride around. By the time we had got down to Banff they decided to take us to the town rubbish dump to see the bears scavenging for odd scraps of food. They then promised to show us a few more things the next day.

They then took us to a park in which there was a collection of buffalo, mountain sheep, elks and bears. When I gave an apple to one of the bears it immediately ate it. I was told that the bears were, in the autumn, very fond of the wild berries. We were also taken to a lake called Minnewanka, around which there were great stands of poplar trees all decked out with amber leaves that gave a splendid splash of colour to the mountainsides. After having lunch in the Banff Springs Hotel that overlooked the Bow valley, we all had a swim in the Sulphur Pool before visiting the museum there, that had an excellent collection of Native American relics. A tumbling stream ran along the floor of a valley and it was there that the young men came to undergo gruelling tests that, when accomplished, qualified them as braves of their tribe.

After a final meal with Rolly and Bunny we said goodbye to them and thanked them very much for the amount of time that they had spent showing us around the Banff area.

On the following morning we took the Calgary road, with the 85 miles journey in front of us. At first we did not get a ride, so we sat down on some roadside low bushes of whortle berries for ten minutes. When we got up we found our khaki trousers badly stained with berry juice. As we looked downhill there appeared a long and heavy freight train labouring uphill into the Kicking Horse Pass with a tall column of writhing black smoke rising into the sky. I managed to get a good photo of this train; it appeared next year in the London and North Eastern Railway's magazine.

As soon as the train had gone, we walked out onto the road again, and almost immediately a car pulled up. The driver said that he was going direct to Calgary and off we went.

The land between the Rockies and Calgary is mostly given over to large ranches, but, with severe spring frosts that only oats can stand, this crop is usually harvested green. We were not so long before we arrived in Calgary, and in 1942 this was a fine city of some 50,000 inhabitants. There were many fine buildings to be seen. We stayed at the YMCA for one dollar a night. At night the city streets were one great blaze of light from advertisements. We had a meal in a Chinese-run cafe and indeed western Canada was littered with these Chinese-run cafes. We ate a meal of fried red salmon, followed by raisin pie and coffee for only 45 cents. The evening was spent in a cinema.

Next day we went to the zoological gardens, where I saw my first grizzly bear, a huge great brute, with thick brown hair with white on its shoulders something like a badger's coat. During our trip along the Rockies we were frequently told about how these bears roamed the distant mountain valleys and how they were liable to attack on sight. One man said that they would prefer to go for women rather than men, if they had a choice.

On the following day we again took to the road, this time to Lethbridge, which was quite a way down south. We were soon picked up by a large car, in which were an elderly undertaker, a middle-aged woman nurse, and a man of the Mounted Police who was driving the car. They told us that they were returning after taking a mental patient to a hospital 150 miles north of Calgary. Mrs Mee, the nurse, said that recently she had befriended an RAF boy who had stolen her gas coupons whilst she was making him a cup of tea in her kitchen.

The car stopped at a place called McLeod outside the undertaker's funeral parlour , and the undertaker said, 'I must see if I have got anybody.' He was soon back saying, 'Yes, I have got old Billy, who was the biggest farmer in the district. He died this morning and he has still got his boots on. 'I'll have to come back, open the jugular vein and pump the blood into a bucket before pumping in about three gallons of embalming fluid.' Sorry if this reads like a lot of butchery, but things had not changed much since the days of the ancient Egyptians and their embalmers.

We got to Lethbridge, where we found that the YMCA was full and we had to take a room for the night at the Palace Rooms that were located over a block of shops near the post office.

A fattish lady in the office told us, 'No drinking or bringing in of women friends is permitted, the boss would not allow it.'

He may have been somewhat religious, because there were several religious tracts on the dressing table. In the lounge there was a notice, 'This lounge is not a lounging place,' and another notice read, 'The lavatory door must not be slammed and there must be no noise after 10.00 p.m.' On the back of our room door was another notice with five verses of poetry giving advice on how to behave in hotels. I have no reason to believe that we gave any offence at all.

Some time earlier a friend of Frank's at 38 SFTS at Estevan had given him the address of a Mr and Mrs Maister who lived in 11th Street at Lethbridge and suggested that we might call on them. That evening we did so and found them living in a large wooden house that had an outside veranda. We were well received and Mr Maister told us a lot about aircraft, and also about the Rockies. He felt that the war would go on for another two years and in this respect he was about right. As a special treat Mrs Maister took two wild duck out of her fridge and roasted them for our suppers. Previously, I had always understood that wild duck tasted of mud, but that was not so with these duck because they tasted so good that I have never forgotten them. Mrs

Maister said the taste came from all the wild rice and farmer's grain eaten whilst in Canada.

At Lethbridge our hitch-hiking was over. In the morning we caught the 9.00 a.m. train to Medicine Hat. Somebody somewhere or other had told me that in Medicine Hat there lived a man named Sairs who, as a part-time interest from his cobbler's business, caught rattlesnakes. A policemen directed us to his shop. In the window there was a large glass case labelled 'Fry's Chocolate'. In this case there were four large rattlesnakes, of which the largest was about five feet long. Each snake had a brownish coloured back, marked by deeper patches and, in my opinion, they were ugly great brutes. When I tapped gently upon the shop window glass, the rattle of the large snake stood up about the size of my middle finger in the centre of its coils and shook like mad. Its seven rings indicated that it was 7 years old. The cobbler said that the dry and rather barren area north-west of the town was infested with these snakes. On the previous Sunday he and another man had caught and killed no fewer than 102 rattlesnakes. The skins were sold into the skin markets. Several people came up and stopped to hear what was being said and one man said that these snakes can give a bite for about half their own length. They strike out for as far as they can reach. One man said that so long as you can see them they are not really dangerous, for they give you warning by their rattles. Another man said that these snakes strike with the same action as the paw of a cat, that leaves long cuts in the flesh. A teenager who happened to come up joined in by saying that on their farm each year they had two or three horses or cattle die of rattlesnake bites.

By this time Frank was getting a bit tired of this review of natural history, so we thanked all concerned and left the cobbler's shop. Frank said that he would go to the Hostess Club and do a bit of reading, whilst I went off along the South Saskatchewan River. I found that it was a broad and swift flowing river. Walking back through the town I passed along a street where the houses had pretty and well-tended gardens and, in one instance, there were several tomato plants that had a lot of ripe tomatoes on them. That evening we caught the night express of the CP Railway to Moose Jaw and from there we picked up another train that stopped at all stations to Estevan. In the yards of some stations there were piles of old and rusty farm machinery waiting to go away for scrap. At one place I saw a steam traction engine at work. It was the only one that I saw doing so on a farm in Canada.

At about two in the afternoon we were back in Estevan, where we both went into the Bakery Cafe for an early tea before catching a bus back to No.38 SFTS. One of the first things that we were told was that while we had been away they had had a six inch fall of snow.

I reckoned that, on this trip, we had by train and by hitching, travelled about 1700 miles all told. My total expenses were about $60, or about £20.00

12

No.38 SFTS Carries on with its Training Programme

When we came back from our holiday in the Rockies we found that several changes had been made. The daily routine orders laid down that the flag square and the road between the stores buildings were now attention areas. All personnel using these areas must now walk 'at attention', also, everyone passing the RAF Ensign must salute it. Doubtless all these measures were standard RAF practice and discipline.

In spite of all these things, to my mind the work of the station went on quite well. At one time it became the practice for many chaps working on the flights that as soon as they had pushed in their own aircraft at evening they promptly set about doing their own daily inspections and left the rest to manage as best they could. But all that had been put right. Another rule that was introduced placed a limit of three aircraftmen working on the flight areas outside each of the hangars. The other chaps were to be employed upon cleaning or repairing aircraft inside the hangars.

At one of the 8.00 a.m. Sunday morning services, or church parades as they called them, Group Captain Cummings, who was the commanding officer of the station, read the lesson of the prodigal son. A few weeks later the padre, Squadron Leader Ashley, advised the old song, 'Praise the Lord and pass the ammunition'.

There were always plenty of opportunities for flying, both for joyrides as well as compulsory when testing aircraft after repairs. One Sunday morning Sergeant Finch took me up in No.8558 for the purpose of an engine test. Although it was a windy day, flying was not at all bumpy. We sailed low over the little prairie farms with their windmills spinning merrily in the west wind. On another occasion Pilot Officer Johnson took Chunky Forstead and myself up on a test flight with No.8562. I had the co-pilot's seat, that gave me a lovely view ahead. At 4,000 feet we flew through light cloud and then came down quite close to the ground. There were three of four crows sitting on the now lifeless branches of some white-branched poplar trees. Johnson dived at these birds, turning the plane so low at 150 m.p.h. that I was pretty sure the port wing tip almost knocked off one of the branches, or one of the crows. I mention these close shaves because I am fairly certain that several of the aircraft accidents we had were due to this low flying.

It was now early November and the first introduction to winter weather was several light falls of powdery snow and if we chanced to remark to any Canadians that it was jolly cold, they invariably replied, 'This is not really cold weather, just you wait until it gets really cold.'

We observed Armistice Day with a general parade of most men and officers. Whilst this was in progress, flying went on all the time, with the result that the noise of the planes almost drowned out the officers' commands.

There was now ice on all the prairie sloughs and I was able to do some skating. As at home, Christmas celebrations and preparations appeared early. Over the radio we heard over and over again, Bing Crosby singing those catchy wartime songs, such as 'The Easter Parade', or 'I'm Dreaming of a White Christmas'. The daylight hours were generally bright with cirrus clouds high in the sky and with dirty clouds a few hundred feet below them. Now and again small flakes of snow fell from nowhere, and they bounced off the dry and frosty ground or the dead prairie grasses. To anyone who stopped for a moment and glanced around the landscape, there was nothing much to see other than the snow-covered fields for endless miles. As I have mentioned earlier, the farmers used to blow the straw from the threshing machines into great heaps that, in midwinter, stood up like small pyramids with their white snow-covered sides.

After tea one day, I took a walk outside the station gate. The moon was rising with an orange-coloured look about it, as it came out of a dark black cloud in the east. Flashes of winter lightning came out behind the cloud. I was bitterly cold and I had to put the ear flaps of my winter cap down before my ears got frozen over. On the next day, when Corporal Lacey and myself were told to go outside on to the flight area in order to put the engine cowlings on the engines of an Anson aircraft, my hands and my face felt scalded, although I was not cold in my body. We had ice cream for tea that day.

It was now December and the weather introduced itself by coming in with the coldest day so far. In Saskatoon the temperature was down to −20F. At Estevan tractors were out in force scraping the snow from runways and finally rolling the surfaces into smooth running. As each plane took off, it left behind a small cloud of swirling snow. On two occasions we had to push the aircraft back into the hangars owing to the fact that the general visibility was so poor.

In spite of all this cold weather, I must admit that we all had good winter clothing, in the form of thick underclothing, leather gloves, hooded jackets and snow boots.

13

A Forced Landing in the USA

Friday 4 December 1942 was a very cold day and I was in the barracks at 6.30 p.m. when Flight Sergeant Smith came in and told me that I was detailed to a small party of men who had to go and be the night guard on plane No.8572 that had made a forced landing abut ten miles inside North Dakota, USA. I immediately went to the cookhouse where Corporal Lacey and a rigger named Guest were already selecting food and drink for our night out. No questions were asked, and we had what we wanted. We next went to the general stores where we picked up sleeping bags, engine covers and so on. We were then taken in one of the stations's cars, the driver of which had already been with two officers to locate the plane. We found it about ten miles over the border west of Noonan. The plane had come down in a large stubble field that had a covering of about four inches of snow on it. At about 8.30 p.m. the station car left us and we set about unloading our gear and food in the cabin of the plane. The cabin thermometer showed a temperature of about −18C.

Corporal Lacey had brought with him a small primus stove, so he immediately set about trying to cook some sausages for our supper. The stove would not light up, so I went off to a row of houses in the next field for some hot water. At the first two houses the ladies said that their stoves were banked down ready for tomorrow's cooking, but at the third house I did get some hot water. We next found that our grapefruit juice, the bread and apples were all frozen solid. We just managed, using a knife, to get condensed milk to flow at a trickle.

It was quite a large field in which the plane had come down, and it was facing south. Apart from the outlines of some surface workings for brown coal, the night scenery around us was nothing more than a white picture of snow-covered prairie country – and very bitterly cold. Then, quite suddenly, we heard the sound of voices and a bunch of about ten boys and girls appeared out of the darkness. Two of the girls handed us an iced plum cake, which they said that their mothers had made and sent us as a present. How very nice of these two ladies. This party then went home. At about 10.00 p.m. another party of about a dozen teenage girls and chaps turned up. They said that they had been skating on what they called The Dam. Each of these girls was dressed very prettily in gaily coloured shawls and trousers that gave a winter sports atmosphere to the snow bound scene.

After these girls had gone we started to think about how we should find room inside the plane's cabin for the three of us to sleep. Then, at about 11.00 p.m. a car arrived in the field with several fellows in it. They offered us some whisky and then pushed off. Corporal Lacey first tried to lie down beside the pilot's seat, but there were too many rudder controls at floor level so he moved back to a place near the main spar. Guest, who had found that the rear gunner's turret was too small for him, now squeezed in beside Lacey. By this time I had decided to take the small space beside the co-pilot's seat, although there was not much space there. Each of us had brought a sleeping bag, also some moccasin boots for sleeping in. We did, of course, have to sleep in our uniforms, as well as throwing our overcoats over us. None of us was reasonably comfortable, but we were cold and settled down to make the best of it. The inside of the plane's cabin was, of course, as cold as an ice house.

At 9.00 a.m. we got up to find that our food had frozen as hard as blocks of ice. We did our best with eating what we could. At 9.30 a.m. Sergeant Hillard, an electrician, Squadron Leader Phillips and Wing Commander Clarke arrived in a motor van. The two officers had come for the purpose of flying the machine back to No.38 SFTS.

Sergeant Hillard then tried to start the engines, but neither of them would offer the least intention of starting. We changed the sparking plugs, primed the engines with petrol until, although petrol was running in a stream out of the exhaust pipes, there was not the slightest response. The engines were as cold as could be, and defied any response. Wing Commander Clarke, head of the engineering side at Estevan, then told the three of us who had been with the plane all night, to get into his car. He took us to Noonan where we went into the hotel for a breakfast that cost the usual 45 cents, at the expense of the RAF. This gesture was, of course, very generous and I think that he could see that we had had a rough night out. After this, he returned to the Estevan base, telling us that he would return with another party equipped with engine covers and heaters. Meanwhile, we all carried on with unsuccessful attempts, until the starboard engine spluttered and restarted.

At 4.00 p.m. the relief party arrived with an electric battery truck, more sparking plugs and a few odd tools. By priming at the rate of about 60 pumps on the primers, the port engine did start. By this time my fingers were terribly cold from continually changing the spark plugs without gloves on my hands, for it was impossible to change these plugs whilst wearing the thick winter gloves that the RAF provided for us. As it was now dark, it was decided to leave the plane in the field for the night and come again in the morning. Whether or not a new night guard was arranged, I never knew.

The three of us, who had been out there for 20 hours, were then taken to the Noonan Hotel, where we were given a lovely hot tea. What a treat it was to have hot water in which to wash our hands, but immediately I put my hands into it, a strange sensation ran through my fingers. Next morning I knew that I had frostbite, and reported sick. At first the MO was rather cross with me, saying that all personnel had been warned to take care. When I explained the circumstances of a night out in a field and how I had put my hands into hot water at the hotel, he then said that putting my hands into that hot water had probably saved them from serious damage. He went on to tell me that I must, at the first opportunity, go into Estevan and buy myself a pair of very light gloves that I could use in the future for changing spark plugs out of doors. The MO then gave me the day off, with light duties only for the following two days. For two days my fingers were very white, but they gradually righted themselves. In a few days my hands were OK again.

On 21 December, the MO, an RCAF man, gave 200 of us a lecture on how to cope with Canadian winter weather. We were told to keep exposed limbs covered up to prevent frostbite. Instead of using the oft-quoted remedy of rubbing frost bites in snow – just let the affected parts thaw out steadily. Snow blindness is another trouble of the prairies and is caused by a certain amount of diet deficiency.

Real winter now set in, and soon the temperature was down to –35F. This cold weather led to trouble with the engines. We had big ignition drops and frozen oil pressure gauges. We were now in midwinter weather all right.

14

Winter Weather and Discipline

During early December it was often a case of touch and go with flying, due to the intermittent snowfall making it unfit for the planes to go up. It was not a case of heavy falls of snow, but that what came down held up the flying programme. For us mechanics it meant that the weather was so cold that it was not possible to leave the machines outside for long periods, because the engines got so cold that they were difficult to restart. This winter weather often meant that we only had about half the usual number of machines in the air. One result was that we were well-advanced with maintenance work and sometimes chaps were waiting for work.

This situation led to another complaint by the engineer officer that he had found men standing about. He said that a visiting group captain had noticed men idling about. Three airmen who were found resting in a crew room were punished by five days in 'jankers'. This led to several men putting in written applications for their transfer to another station. According to rumour, they said that they were tired of being buggered about. About two days afterwards Flight Lieutenant Wright came into one of the hangars threatening to make all fitters remove the engine cowlings during daily inspections and he did look really cross. One of the flight sergeants told me to nip round the hangar and tell all the other chaps to take off their cowlings before this officer got to them.

During that afternoon the discontents were taken to the commanding officer, but for some good reason he declined to see them. However, we heard, rightly or wrongly, that the CO had spoken rather sharply to Flight Lieutenant Wright. Afterwards the six men were seen individually by Wing Commander Clarke. It seems that the men were given a promise that a re-organization would take place and some improvements made on the station.

In spite of all these troubles, the situation did not stop preparations for Christmas. In the dining hall there was already a ten foot high Christmas tree in position.

A few days before Christmas the officers and NCOs of No.4 Hangar gave each man a hundred Players cigarettes as a Christmas present. They must have been appreciative of the work and results of the airmen's endeavours, or they would not have been so kind. A Christmas leave of five days was announced. One half of the personnel would take the five days at Christmas and the other half would have five days at the New Year.

15

Christmas in Canada 1942

Many Canadian families, some near and some hundreds of miles away, had agreed to take RAF airmen who would care to join them in their homes for Christmas. All personnel at No.38 SFTS were advised before Christmas and I put my name down in acceptance, with the result that a Mr and Mrs Macelhouse would accept Walter Torrington and myself at their home in Winnipeg for the Christmas holiday. Walter was an airframes mechanic, who before being called up was employed as the gardener to a wealthy and retired brewer in Stockport in Lancashire. He was younger than myself and, although we did not know each other particularly well, he was a good companion for the trip. We left on Christmas Eve by the 7.15 a.m. train that stopped at all stations to Winnipeg. As we passed along in the train it seemed as if the snow-covered prairie stretched endlessly. There were several places where the train stopped for about an hour. Most passengers got down and walked a short distance into the town where they had a meal in one of the cafes. Walter and I did the same thing. Canadian policemen walking the streets wore black fur caps. At 8.30 p.m. we arrived in Winnipeg, where we found the station concourse gaily decorated with all manner of coloured lights and streamers.

Mr Macelhouse, our host, saw us standing alone, and came up to me asking, 'Are you Mr Torkington?' He had with him another man called Eric and we were soon whisked away in a car.

The streets of Winnipeg were one great blaze of light and there were Christmas trees in some streets, as well as in many house front gardens. These trees were, for the most part, standing in blocks of ice. We stopped at a brewery to buy a barrel of beer which we left at Eric's home.

The Macelhouses had a lovely big house built of wood, and detached. Mrs Macelhouse then met us and we saw that she was a fine, well-dressed woman, probably 40 years old, and a very nice lady. They had three children, Dick, Fred and a little girl called Mary Jane. We had coffee before going to Eric's home for a Christmas Eve party. Several people sang songs, or recited poems with a sexual flavour which were, by British standards, perhaps rather explicit.

On Christmas morning the children were up early and they soon took their Christmas presents from a Christmas tree standing in the living room. The two boys had dark brown skiing trousers, whilst Mary Jane had a smart new night-gown decorated with blue smocking.

During the afternoon we talked about books, British and American ways of life and the Canadian weather. At about 6.00 p.m. we all sat down to a splendid Christmas dinner. There was a huge, well-cooked turkey, with mashed potatoes, mashed parsnips, gravy and cranberry jelly. For a sweet we had a Christmas pudding well filled with fruit and flavoured with wine. After supper the children all went to bed, whilst we adults went to a nearby house, to a family by the name of Harper. They had two teenage children named Jimmy and Brenda, who were very sociable by playing a game of cards with Walter and me. It was in this house that I saw for the first time a red-leafed plant called a poinsettia. After the war this plant became a popular Christmas decoration in Britain.

The Macelhouse house was quite a large one, and very comfortably furnished. Like most Canadian houses, it had a large cellar, with a heating boiler in it. There were so many copper pipes in this cellar that one felt that one was in the boiler room of a steamship. I think that this boiler was gas-fired and that the heat generated was circulated as hot air all over the house.

On the following day we were taken by car on a tour of the town by Mr Macelhouse. In the Assiniboine Park we saw children playing on skates, or on snowshoes. We also saw the confluence of the Assiniboine and Red Rivers, both of them frozen over. In the town streets we also saw several horse-drawn vehicles on sleigh runners. To me all these sights made Winnipeg into a dream city, all very white and frostbound.

Next day we sat indoors, talking about dozens of subjects until almost midnight. The following day was our last one in Winnipeg, when we were taken to the station for the 10.25 a.m. train to Estevan. We said our fond goodbyes to the very kind people who had entertained us so royally all over Christmas.

The last thing I did before getting into the train, was to take a photo of a preserved steam locomotive CPR No. 1, outside the station. A plate on the engine read, 'The first locomotive to be used in Western Canada. It was brought on a barge up the Red River in 1877'. As I stood by the engine the wind was bitterly cold; it nipped my ears terribly. Never before had I felt such a bitter wind.

As we travelled home in the train across the prairies, the wind blew snow and dust across the line in clouds, like a thick mist.

It was late evening by the time we arrived back in Estevan.

16

The War Situation in 1943

The progress of the war in 1943 was much better than it had been a year ago. This did not mean that we were riding entirely high, although we were now beginning to see signs that we were starting to hold our own.

The arrival of General Montgomery in North Africa had seen the German Africa Corps steadily held and in many instances pushed back. In November we had taken no fewer than 80,000 Italian prisoners of war. From Russia there was good news saying that the German armies were now falling back from Stalingrad. These bits of favourable news began to make many airmen feel that the end of the war was in sight. The Americans had advanced in North Africa, whilst their navy had sunk several Japanese warships in the Pacific. The Americans were now singing a new song, 'We will remember Pearl Harbor as we did the Alamo'. When we first arrived at Estevan nearly a year ago, a party of American schoolgirls came to us and sang this song.

We were still losing quite a few ships by submarine attacks in the Atlantic. Two American vessels had been sunk with the loss of about 850 lives, both civilian and service personnel. At this time we had not got our intelligence service up to the peak that it was later on in the year, when we were able to fool the Germans with duff information about the position of convoys and we were soon able to deal more effectively with the location of German submarines and their destruction. The winning of the Atlantic campaign against German submarines was one of the telling factors in our favour.

A little later on I was the victim of an April Fool's Day prank made by a chap named Taffy. I was awakened at 5.15 a.m. by one of the station police who acted on a false notice that I was required to report for 'jankers'. I signed the sheet, and went to sleep again. On the same day I received a letter from my wife Hilda saying that she was now recovering from an attack of pneumonia and that the Air Ministry had cancelled all arrangements made for her to come out to Canada. The reason for this change of policy was lack of space to bring back families after their RAF men had been brought back to Great Britain. Hilda seemed disappointed, but there it was.

17

Catching up on Delays due to Christmas Leave and Snowfalls

The falls of snow and the Christmas leave interrupted the pilot training programme quite considerably. Whenever it snowed, planes went up, but they were frequently prevented from flying for very long, with the result that things got behindhand somewhat and we had to cope with new rules about discipline and dress. Flight Sergeant Smith told us that in future we had to come to work in blue uniform and change into overalls in the hangar. At the finish of work we must leave our overalls in the hangar and walk back in blue uniform. We also must have polished buttons on our work tunics. Our new CO sounds a bit strict, for at a barrack inspection he told an airman that his buttons were dirty.

One day I forgot that there was a morning inspection parade. Squadron Leader Glenny looked over me, and pointing to my boots said that they were dirty.

The Adjutant said to me, 'You have not polished those boots lately.'

I replied, 'I'm afraid, sir, that they are full of engine oil,' to which he said, 'You must, for this parade, put on your best boots.'

At this, the two officers moved on. I heard nothing more about it at all.

About a month later I was due for 48 hours leave and I had a chit to finish work at 12.00 noon on the Friday. However, Sergeant Fernaux said that I had better stop back in order to see that the engines of a certain plane upon which I had carried out an inspection, were all right for an afternoon flight. When I went back, Flight Sergeant Horner made me fly with the plane. We had a pilot named Dougall Black, who was a proper daredevil. Once, in the air, he caught up with another machine, probably by prior private arrangement to engage in a proper mock dogfight. We had the wing tips screaming as he lifted and dived, turned steeply, stalled, and goodness only knows what else he did with the plane. Half the time my heart was in my mouth.

Sergeant Cutler, a flying instructor in No.6 Hangar, is to be Court Martialled for unauthorized low flying over a prairie lake, where Wing Commander Clarke happened to be lying in wait for wild ducks. No doubt Clarke was annoyed at the way his ducks were driven off.

Whenever it did not snow, the planes went up and everything seemed to be normal, but there were still grouses about the training programme being behind.

At our work on the engine maintenance, we fitters seemed to work as much as we could. One January day I was working on the port engine of Anson 8549. There was an ignition drop of 150 r.p.m. when switched on to battery only. After a deal of fiddling about I thought that I had got it all right, but when we took the plane out we found that the starboard engine now had a 250 r.p.m. drop when switched on to magneto only. The crew arrived to take the plane up at about 4.00 p.m., but we had to give it up for the day. That was how things used to go, but we had to do a good job and there were no chances of dodging good workmanship.

On one of those January days there was what was called a 'sun dog', or a sort of halo around the sun. Previously I had seen this feature once in England. In Canada it is more common.

In February I was put into No.6 Hangar for further experience as a fitter. I was put with Fitter Rickards, an insurance agent in civvy life, with whom I had already made an acquaintance. He had already made several long distance hitch-hikes. In fact, he had put into my head the idea of going to the southern part of the USA. We got on well enough together at work. Ricky was a great planner of long hitch-hikes and he could plan the details perfectly.

House sparrows are birds that had adapted themselves very well to life in the Canadian winter. We had a twice daily visit of a mobile canteen to the hangars. Immediately the doors were opened to let the canteen wagon enter, about 20 or 30 of these birds got very excited and flew down in readiness to peck up any crumbs dropped by the airmen. During the coldest part of the winter these sparrows lived permanently in the hangar.

It so happened that in our hangar we were waiting for work due to late delivery of engine bearer mount rings. These rings held the engine in position, but due to the intense vibration to which they were subjected, the brackets had a tendency to fracture. During inspections I did find several broken bracket lugs, but I do not recall that an engine actually fell off in the air.

During the evening of 4 April 1943 there was celebrated the first anniversary of No. 38 SFTS. Several hundred airman and officers gathered in the drill hall for a dance and a drinking session. A party of girls from Winnipeg came and sang us a few songs. Group Captain Lea-Cox went to the microphone to make a short speech, but he was unfortunately stopped from doing so by an airman who had taken a lot of drink.

18

A Likeable Chap Who Was an Incorrigible Rogue

It seems time that something of a comic interlude should be mentioned. We had a Welshman among us. He was an engine mechanic and he was in our barrack room. He was well-known as the most plausible rogue imaginable – yet he was liked by everyone, even if he owed them money. He even owed me a dollar and I never got it back, nor did I really mind because I was repaid by hearing of Taffy's antics.

What Taffy used to do was to get in touch with firms that supplied goods and delivered them for payment on delivery. He almost always limited his calls on chaps to one dollar. He sent details to the people who supplied the goods and just put the money into his own pocket. The next thing that the chaps who had paid their dollars heard was a notice from the Estevan post office that a Montreal firm of shoemakers had supplied a pair of shoes, and that they could have them by coming down and paying four dollars for the shoes. It seems that Taffy had collected a dollar from several of the trainee pilots and I think it was some of them who were due for recall to Great Britain, and chaps who did not know Taffy particularly well reported the matter to the station warrant officer. The outcome of all this was that Taffy did several days in the guardroom. After Christmas he drank rather heavily and did not go to work for several days, until the flight lieutenant who was engineer officer caught up with him. Taffy told me that he swore at this officer and said that he did not care a toss for him and so on. He was then put back into the guardroom where he pleaded nervous strain. He was then sent to a specialist doctor in Edmonton and when he came back he told me that he had been subjected to some kind of electrical gadget put on his head while he was asked questions. Every time the doctor asked him to put his hands up or down, Taffy did just the opposite. In other words, he was trying to feign that he was a nutcase.

After he came back to Estevan the commanding officer saw Taffy and told him that he had been recommended for a transfer back to England. However, for the charges made against him, it would mean confinement to the station for 14 days and the cancellation of all privileges during that period. Further, he was told, or so he said, that he would be posted back to Britain within a month. As it happened, he was still with us a year later.

In addition to the boots incident Taffy was also involved with a scheme to supply an Estevan person with some car tyres. An arrangement was made whereby the man must leave his house window open at night so that Taffy could come along and just push the tyres inside. Although the man paid his money for these promised tyres, I do not think that he ever got them.

19

Wild Flowers, Animals and Wild Fruit

Very early on I noticed that there was a great variety of wild flowers, so I started a collection of dried wild flowers. At Regina I bought a book on wild flowers of Canada, together with a proper book in which to store my dried specimens. In 1944, when I returned to Britain, I brought back with me a collection of about 150 specimens. Many of these flowers were not of Canadian origin, but specimens of European flowers whose seeds had been brought over as 'hitch-hikers' in bags of seed corn and so on. Of all the flowers that I collected, I think that the one I liked best was a red lily. It was known as the western red lily and it was the emblem of Saskatchewan. I think that I only saw two specimens of the western red lily, and sometime afterwards I was told by an Englishman that it was at heart a British native flower.

Of wild fruits there was not a great collection. There was a small red gooseberry found on waste places about the prairie. A bush that grew to a height of about six feet produced a plum-like fruit known as choke cherry and I did eat some of these fruits. So far as I can recall, I never met any of our European blackberries. At work, we had a morning and afternoon break for 15 minutes, when a NAAFI wagon toured the hangars. In summer, as we sat on the ground, we saw small wild tomato plants growing out of the soil, but the tomatoes were only as big as peas.

Each spring a great variety and quantity of birds migrated up from the southern USA into Canada. So far as I could see, none of these birds stayed in Canada over the bitter winters, but I was never quite sure. I did read that a bird known as a prairie chicken, which was about the size of a British partridge, had strange habits. Apparently, during the autumn it started to disappear from certain places, to congregate in great numbers in others. Instead of going south, these birds flew north. Up there they managed, on the semi-barren areas just below the Arctic, to live on the frozen bilberries and the buds of certain trees.

There was one bird known as a sap sucker because, like a woodpecker, it pecked holes in the trees and sucked out from the bark enough sap to live on. Whilst helping a farmer with his harvest, he showed me a grass field in which there was a great number of small holes about two inches in diameter. He told me that a small owl lived in these holes, but I never found out whether these owls overwintered in Canada.

There were no poisonous snakes in the Estevan area. We did have a small snake called a garter snake, because it had a long golden stripe all along each side of its green body.

There were a few wild animals, of which the most common was called a gopher. It was a light cream, weasel-like rodent that lived in deep holes that it dug for itself on the prairie. These little animals had the habit of sitting bolt upright above the entrance to their burrows, as they watched people approaching. They hibernated in winter.

The odd rabbit might be seen, but they were not numerous in and around Estevan. There was a sort of large hare that was known as a Jack rabbit. A small wolf known as a coyote lived on the prairies. They were hunters of the night that could be heard howling about the farmlands. They did not attack human beings. On one occasion I met a farmer riding on horseback who stopped and had a chat with me. He said that in winter he turned his horses loose on the prairie and left them to look after themselves. As the farmers left their straw blown into high heaps, these loose horses had a habit of getting into the straw heaps and rolling about in the straw. Sometimes the horses got upside down and could not right themselves. He had been to see if any of his horses had got into such a fix. He went on to say that the horse under him, and I thought that it looked a fine horse too, would be shot soon. He would then strip the skin and the carcass would be dumped outside the barn, where it would soon be frozen stiff and left to the coyotes who would gradually gnaw it down to a few big bones during the winter.

In the Souris River there were a few big turtles that might be seen occasionally paddling up or down the stream. There were no beavers in the Estevan area, but in the north of Saskatchewan where there are better and bigger rivers that suited these animals, beavers were to be found. In a newspaper I read that a woman had been prosecuted for buying a beaver skin from a Native American and trying to sell it during the closed season. She pleaded that the Native Americans had been compelled to kill the beavers for food. In that case, the judge ruled that the woman was guilty, because the pelt should have been taken to a government office for sale.

Of insects, we were plagued with mosquitoes, for they bit us unmercifully. On the first weekend leave that we had, both Frank Dowell and myself went to Regina with faces very red and bloated by mosquito bites. These mosquitoes bit any exposed part of our flesh. They sucked out blood until they were as bloated as a small blue balloon. So heavy were they with this load of blood that it was only with difficulty that they kept in the air. In time, most chaps came to put up with this nuisance, which lasted only in the summer months.

20

Miscellaneous Matters

My wife, Hilda, who was still teaching in the Hereward School in March, wrote regularly to me. In her letter written in September 1942 she said how she had been taking parties of schoolgirls to pick plums in fields near Wisbech. This was an organized fruit picking expedition, that was regarded as war work, and on one occasion they had picked no less than four and a half tons of plums in one day.

Whilst mentioning a farming pursuit may I say that I went, during the late summer of 1942, to visit a threshing scene quite close to our airfield and just over the Souris River to the west of the airfield. A tractor provided the power for this communal barley threshing and the barley sheaves were led in two-horse wagons to the machine that stood in the middle of the field. The tractor had been made by the firm of Jerome Increase Case at Racine, USA, and was owned by an Englishman named Blackburn, and an all metal threshing machine was owned by an Armenian. This machine was quite modern, for it cut the sheaf bands automatically, and delivered the threshed grain through a side pipe that shot it out at the rate of one bushel a time. In this case, it actually delivered the grain through a side pipe onto the ground. Two Frenchmen were picking up the sheaves from the stooks in the field.

Another young chap said, 'I'm a bit of every damn thing.'

The threshed straw was as usual, blown into a tall heap at the rear.

There happened to be another gang working about half a mile away, so I called on them.

The farmer told me that, 'In my opinion, Canada should have been left to the Native Americans.' When I asked him if they ever ploughed up any of their relics, he said, 'Yes, we do find some arrowheads now and again.'

At that time wheat was selling at 72 cents a bushel.

The next day I had lunch with an airman who told me that the fattish sergeant electrician who had been posted back to Britain had been torpedoed at sea and after rescue was brought back to Canada.

Somebody else told me that last Christmas the two corporals in my room had decided to spend the holiday in Regina. They went by train, but whilst changing trains at Moose Jaw they walked into town for a drink. They met two women in a bar, had a lot of drink and then slept with the two pick-ups. When they awoke in the morning, both the women had disappeared and so had all their money. They had to return to Estevan and spent the rest of Christmas in barracks.

21

A Snow Blizzard

Canada is noted for snowstorms and on Saturday 13 March 1943 a blizzard of wind and snow set in and it lasted for five days. It so happened that I was staying in the Empire Hotel in Estevan on the Friday night prior to going to Regina or some such place on the Saturday morning. The onset of snow made travel quite impossible on the Saturday, with the result that I, along with about half a dozen other airmen, was stranded in the hotel. All that day the wind blew at gale force; it piled the snow into drifts up to six feet high all along the town's high street. Along with the other stranded airmen, and one or two Canadians who were also trapped in the hotel, we watched the blizzard through the hotel windows. Canadians in the hotel told us that it was the worst snowstorm they had ever seen. On the Sunday no trains had run and sleighs drawn by horses were the only vehicles that passed.

On Monday the snow still fell and one of the airmen rang up the airfield guardroom telling them of our stranded position. The answer was that, as soon as possible, a tractor-hauled sledge would be sent to fetch us. It did not come, so on the Monday evening another airman and myself struggled through the piled up snow to the town cinema. Only about 50 people turned up at the cinema and all that we saw was one short film at 7.30 p.m. Although the snowstorm began to fade out by Wednesday, neither trains nor much road traffic was able to move. When the promised sledge arrived to take us airmen back to the airfield, it was hauled by a caterpillar tractor. Although the sledge was listed as being able to take a load of four tons, there were so many boxes of foodstuffs and other priority parcels on it that only about half a dozen chaps were able to sit on the top of this conveyance. I was not included as a passenger.

On the Wednesday evening the weather lifted, and the sun came out and shone brilliantly. About a dozen of us decided to walk back to No. 38 SFTS. What a beautifully white world it was.

At the guardroom our names were taken and we were told that we had overstayed our weekend leave; we should expect to have to give a full explanation. In the event, nothing further happened.

22

The Flood that Followed the Snowstorm

About two weeks after this great snowstorm there set in a determined thaw, with the result that the Souris river flooded extensively and wide areas on both sides of the river were put under water. The road between Estevan and the airfield was flooded to such an extent that only a few motor vehicles could get through.

At breakfast time there was a call for volunteers who would help to make the road passable. It so happened that we did not have a lot of work in the hangars, so I put my name down. When we arrived on the scene, several bungalows near Wood Lane Park had already been deserted and water was up to the windowsills. Before leaving the station we were issued with a pair of rubber boots and a wide-bladed shovel.

On arrival at the scene we found that several workmen employed by the roads authority had already started to build up an earth bank on the west side of the road in order that all water going downstream might be prevented from crossing the road and be diverted through the bridge. There were one or two boats already in use and we could use them as we wished. The site of the flooded road was known as Wood Lane Park, which was used as a substitute for a seaside watering place, and since Estevan was distant from the sea by about 1,000 miles, the place was much frequented in summertime. Even folks from the USA used to come there.

I started working on the making of the earth bank intended to prevent the water from crossing the road. What surprised me was the large number of fish that were swimming in shoals over the flooded part of the road. They were all swimming frantically outwards towards the edge of the flood. These green-coloured fish were about the size of British minnows or whitebait. I caught several of these fish in my hands quite easily. As these fish seemed determined to get away from the main stream of the river, I felt that they must have a special reason for doing so. I never solved the mystery of the fishes' movements.

At evening we airmen went back to the station and we learned that the main reason for our going on this special job was because the station's anniversary of its opening was to be held that evening and quite a number of Estevan residents were expected to attend. In the event, they all got through, because the peak of the flood subsided that afternoon. The highways authority did place a prohibition on all vehicles over 6,000 pound weight.

23

In Hospital

About a week after we had cleared up the flood trouble I reported sick with a boil on my behind that would not come to a head. Flight Lieutenant Eaglesham of the RCAF, our MO took me into hospital and ordered hot poultices. Inside the hospital it was very pleasant indeed. Each bed had a white enamel cabinet beside it, and there was brown linoleum over the floor. A splash of colour was provided by a red blanket folded across each bed. Nursing duties were carried out by two RCAF Nurses. There were also two RAF male nurses or orderlies who did most of the routine work in the hospital.

As it was found that the poulticing of my boil did not work, the MO decided that he must lance the boil. I was taken into the operating theatre, where the table was little more than a sort of strengthened, four-legged clothes-ironing table. I was given a local anaesthetic and as the MO picked up his scalpel the operating table collapsed and, bang, I went down on the floor. The two Canadian sisters, Miss Jacques and Miss Maclaren, laughed and thought it was a good joke, which I suppose it was. The table was re-erected and the MO was able to cut the boil open. I was then given hospital blue dress for the duration of my stay. I was given all sorts of jobs, such as polishing the floor of the operating theatre, where I looked at the extensive array of knives or saws for cutting off patients' limbs. In seven days I was let out of the hospital as an outpatient.

Whilst in hospital I found that the Canadian MO was a very pleasant man to deal with. I well remember that he said to me that I should think seriously about buying a bit of land in Canada. As a matter of fact I did so much later on. Canadian officers seemed to come down to a man's level; this I think was part of the one-class American way of life.

24

More Pressure on the Workload at Estevan

As soon as the worst weather of the winter was over there were talks about catching up on the delays to flying training. We were told that it was necessary that new working hours must be introduced. For airmen working in the hangars the days began at 7.30 a.m. and continued until 8.00 p.m. One day no fewer than 500 flying hours were achieved. Even so, we were told that there must be at least ten planes ready to fly each morning and all 48 hour weekend leave was cancelled.

Warrant Officer Green said that one airman had complained about the cancellation of leave, but he had told him that the chaps fighting in Tunisia got no weekend leave at all.

This man had replied, 'That's all very well, but that's over there.'

Green then gave us a pep talk, saying that the hangars were full of planes under repair and overtime might have to be introduced. He told us that our job in Canada was just as important as those on the fighting fronts. If we got bolshie, there was always the guardroom.

At this time Ricky and I were working on a complete engine change on Anson 8584. We had several bits of bother, including a complete retiming of the engine ignition. We stuck at the job, even working until 9.00 p.m. at night. At that time it was the practice to have four engine fitters on each plane; two on one engine and two on the other.

At one time planes were going up and down like the angels in Jacob's dream as related in the Old Testament. Ricky and I had done an engine replacement on plane No. 8438. I had to go on the test flight, sitting in the co-pilot's seat. I found that my parachute was oversized and I think that if I had been obliged to jump out I would have fallen through the harness. We climbed to 5,000 feet, did one or two sharp turns, a speed test as well as give a R.P.M test to the engines. We were flying over Crosby in the USA when the pilot asked me if I would like to fly into the clouds and up we went to 9,500 feet. It was a lovely day for flying, with lots of sunshine and picturesque clouds. That evening I had to work until 9.00 p.m., but one had to take the rough with the smooth.

At this time there were several rumours going around about our future. George Marrs, who worked in the flight office, said that we were likely to be moved into a more active theatre of the war, probably with the Americans, but nothing came of this.

25

The Opening Up of Western Canada and the Native Americans

The Hudson's Bay Company played a large part in the development of Western Canada and the exploitation of the fur trade. They instituted what they called canoe brigades. Each spring these canoe parties set off from the large trading posts in central Canada and ascended the great rivers and chains of lakes. The company split the brigades into three groups: gentlemen, white men and hunters. The gentlemen usually went in pairs – a gentleman and his lieutenant, who were dressed in cocked hats, satin waistcoats, and a pistol somewhere about them, and very often they carried a sword stuck in their high boot legs. These men were given the best places in the canoes, or the best horses in the brigade. The second class were either the servants to dress the skins and cook the meals, or young clerks sent out for training in some future high post. By far the most picturesque of the parties were the motley hunters – Native American half-breeds, and white men in buckskin suits that had hawks' bills hung down the side of their leggings. On the heads of these men were scarves of blue handkerchiefs binding back their dark hair. They also had a bright sash about their waists and moccasins beaded like works of art. Then, often enough, there was a musician in a party, and the sound of 'The Campbells are Coming' was heard drifting through the rocky canyons. Many men took their wives with them. This is perhaps a general picture of the times and I was grateful for this account which I read about somewhere or other. If you go to Jasper, you will see in the mountain paths, memorials to the men who did this pioneering.

The Native Americans did not altogether welcome this intrusion of the white man, although they were ready enough to sell their animal skins to the intruders. On the reverse side, the introduction of alcoholic drink had unfortunate results. Right from the start the white men took Native American wives, who very soon produced a mixed bunch of men with varied characteristics, sometimes not of the best characters. These Native American women used to chew the leather skins for the purpose of making moccasins, for there were no other means of getting footwear.

In general the Native Americans were a cruel race, for one of their practices was to cut off the hair of women in order to get scalps. They cut this hair off with the skin attached and then plastered on an animal's bladder skin, and hoped that the nasty mess would eventually heal.

The Native Americans, of course, had their medicine men. I well recall that in 1943 I read an account in a local paper, giving the experience of an overseer of a Saskatchewan Native American reservation. This man had charge of the Native Americans and he had one man who was dying of double pneumonia. The sick man was convinced that one of his enemies on the reservation, a fellow Native American, had put a painful thing in his chest. A Canadian doctor thought that the sick man would be dead by the time that the overseer called again in a fortnight's time. However, in the event he found to his surprise that the man was sitting up in bed much recovered. Pointing to a box under the bed, he said that a woman medicine man had removed the painful object and it was in that bag.

The Native Americans led a somewhat precarious life, and it often happened, in winter weather, that those who lived in the Labrador area died of starvation whilst on the trail.

It was a Native American belief that there was a great spirit to whom all forms of animal life were acceptable. Those from the west coast were more highly developed. They believed that salmon fish were provided for their benefit and after eating them it was their responsibility to see that no bones were broken, because they buried the fish bones for the salmon to use again in their next life. Many of the old chiefs were annoyed at the present avoidance of this old practice, blaming part of the trouble on the coming of the white man.

Strangely enough, there is a tradition among the Native Americans of a great world flood, similar to the legends of other indigenous peoples in other parts of the world.

In May 1943 I did see my first Canadian Native Americans. I was hitch-hiking in the north of Saskatchewan when a butcher named Coxtan, a tall middle-aged man, spoke to me in the street in a place called Carlyle. He asked me whether I would like to see a Native American reservation at White Bear, a few miles to the north. I immediately accepted the invitation, and, accompanied by Mr Kempton, the town clerk, we were soon swept away in a one-ton motor truck. The reservation was in what they called the Moose Mountains, a district of low hills where some three hundred Indians lived in little wooden huts. There were Native Americans of several tribes, including Assiniboines, Crees, Blackfoot, and Sioux, all living together.

A chief named Wassenages and his squaw ran down a hill to greet us. I gave them 25 cents apiece, for which they seemed very grateful. Both were dressed in European clothes. They immediately showed us inside their little bungalow-type hut. Neither of them spoke but a very few words of English. Inside the hut there was a cat tied to a bed leg, a spaniel and six pups in a box. The iron bedstead had on it a few tousled blankets and a bundle of turkey feathers hung from a roof rafter. In the middle of the hut there stood a large iron stove. Both Native Americans had stone-bowled pipes with 10 inch wooden stems. The old chief pointed to a rabbit skin, saying, 'Wapoose,' which I took for rabbit. The colour of their skin was a brownish copper and they had brown eyes. It did seem to me a sad thing that the remnants of the Native American tribes should now be cooped up in what was something like a concentration camp. What the government did in the way of financial help I never knew.

When we came away, Mr Kempton and I went into a Chinese run cafe in Carlyle for a meal. The proprietor told me that he had two sons, one of whom had been killed in the raid on Dieppe and the other in the crash of a Wellington bomber in Malta.

It was whilst reading an American magazine a little later on, that I came across an account of how, when a USA cave was opened up, it contained the mummified body of a Native American miner, who had been dressed in woven garments. There were also traces of a rush torch. From the position of this man's body it would appear that he had been trapped by a fall of rock. It was very likely that this man belonged to some ancient civilization about which little or nothing was now known.

So far as the Native American languages were concerned, I learned but two or three words only. A lonesome pine tree was called a *konananskis* and where clear water flowed over a pebbled bottom with the sun shining on it, I think the word was *kalamazoo*.

The Canadian Native Americans do not appear to have done any cave painting, but on the west coast there are strange outlines of figures or inscriptions on large stones. If you go into some museums on the coast of British Columbia there are to be seen examples of these carvings.

26

More About Flying in the RAF

On Thursday 27 May 1943 I was on a test flight with Pilot Officer Bancroft on Anson 8583. We had done an overall inspection on this plane. With us was a very young airframes fitter who had never before been up in a plane, but after a lot of persuasion from his mates he agreed to come on this trip. When we were in the air the pilot found that he could not get an indication that the undercarriage was locked in the up position, so he asked me to get the airframes man to come forward and have a word with him. I turned to the nearest man behind me in the plane and asked him to get the rigger to come to the front. But the chap had gone to the farthest place back that he could possibly find and refused to budge.

When I told the pilot that the fellow would not come forward, he replied, 'Never mind, I will try and fix things up. I am going to do a steep dive and then pull out of it, in the hope that this will fix it. Tell everybody to hold fast.'

There was a resounding bump as we hit the air with a loud bang, for the air seemed as solid as a bit of rock, but the indicator still showed no indication of a locked position. The pilot then had another go, but with no result.

'I shall now have to do an emergency landing, but with the permission of the ground control.'

He radioed with the control tower and a path was given to us. We made a very shallow approach, and passed over the boundary fence only a few feet above it. We touched down very gently and the undercarriage held up.

However, that was not the end of the matter, because as soon as we had started our next job on another aircraft, a flight sergeant came up with a young engineer officer. 'This is Bonnett, who was the senior aircraftman on the plane,' said the flight sergeant. The officer asked me what had happened, and I told him the story. 'Well,' he said, 'do you realize that the skin coverings of the main planes are split and we shall in all probability find that the main spars are either cracked or broken. I shall hold you responsible and you will find yourself on a charge.'

I replied that I did not consider that I, an ordinary aircraftman, could tell a commissioned pilot officer what he should do in the air. He had told us all what he intended to do. Fortunately, I heard nothing further about this matter. As far as the undercarriage was concerned, I should say that all that was wrong with it was that it was actually locked up, but the recording mechanism was at fault.

27

Odds and Ends

During the middle of 1943 a travelling concession was introduced that was a big boon to ordinary airmen. From now on, all those on a 48 hours weekend leave could take advantage of putting their names down at the flying control office for an airlift to any particular SFTS station to which a plane might be going on routine training or other business. If a plane was going on such journeys, well, one could be lucky on a Friday afternoon. I had a ride to Assiniboine SFTS, which was about 150 miles west of Estevan. I decided to hitch-hike back again. I well remember going into the NAAFI canteen at Assiniboine for a coffee and a bun before setting off. I sat at a table opposite a young trainee pilot who was what he called 'cheesed off', due to finding the training a bit too much for him. He had decided that he was not the right chap for flying and would ask to come off the training.

I did not do very well with my hitch-hiking homewards. Lifts were few and far between, and at 9.30 p.m. I found myself stranded at a place called Vantage. The only accommodation available was at a Chinese-owned cafe. My bedroom was rather dingy, with unwashed sheets and a cracked chamber pot. In the morning I paid my bill for about 4/6d and went away without taking breakfast. I took the road to Moose Jaw, some eighty miles to the south. I very soon got a ride, and we passed many farmers buzzing about on tractors and, although it was now the month of June, several fields of last year's wheat were now being cut.

During the next day I set out for Regina, and it was a Russian who was driving the car in which I was given a lift. He was a good conversationalist, and told me that he had in the 1914-18

War served in the Russian army. Before emigrating to Canada he had toured Germany, Poland, Austria and whilst on his way to Canada he had had a look at England.

Whilst mentioning a Russian, could I repeat what a Canadian named Ross, whom I met in the bus to Regina some time previously, said to me about Russian settlers in Canada? According to Mr Ross, Russians did not make the best settlers. In their houses they all slept in one big bed under a wide, thick tick covering. Sometimes the husband finds that his wife has crept up to the hired hand and such situations lead to a brawl or even a murder. All told, there was plenty of disorder and in one small Alberta town it was necessary to have extra mounted police to deal with the Russian population.

Whilst passing the time during the afternoon in a park at Regina I got into conversation with one of the gardeners who was watering the flowers. Never before had this man seen worms in the ground and I had often remarked on this absence. From the park I went to the airfield at Regina, and was allocated a plane ride back to Estevan. Most of the way back the instructor and his pupil were arguing about the way the pupil would not rely upon the instruments only to fly the plane.

On the radio next day there was a report of how an Alberta farmer had been raided by a wild bear that had come out of the woods and killed no fewer than 14 of his hogs. The farmer was furious about it all and the only consolation he had was the fact that he had shot the bear.

There was also a radio report that Winston Churchill had made a speech in the House of Commons about the situation in North Africa. The British casualties in Tunisia had been very heavy, amounting to some 35,000 killed, missing or wounded. So far as the Axis forces were concerned, they had lost around 300,000 men – 50,000 killed, and 248,000 taken prisoner.

Churchill then said, 'I can now see the mellow light of victory.'

At Estevan, the RAF had brightened up the airfield by planting large numbers of trees and shrubs. Around the airmen's mess there were a dozen or more ten foot high trees that look like Christmas trees. One could hardly recognize the place from what it was when we came here eighteen months ago.

Whilst I was walking down to Estevan I saw an insect-eating night hawk. This bird was brownish-looking, with a white strip across each wing. When it flew away, it wheeled about in the manner of a bat. I called in at Wood Lane Park where I noticed that there were masses of violets; many of these flowers had stalks a foot long.

My wife Hilda wrote me a letter saying that the Air Ministry had told her that on 6 April 1944 I would be due for return to Britain.

I had a lift back to the airfield in an American car; the driver of it had been to a conference on grasshopper prevention. I asked him what was the difference between a gopher and a prairie dog. I was told that gophers are smaller than prairie dogs, who live in towns or large mounds. These prairie dogs are found further west in both Canada and the USA.

I had a pleasant little flight with Pilot Officer Outerbridge, a Canadian, in 8575. Whilst over the USA he said to me, 'Take her back.' I immediately looked over my shoulder to catch a sight of the sun. He pointed to the compass. However, I managed, by looking at the instruments, to get back OK, so he let me do one circuit of the airfield.

At the end of June we had a new padre, when Squadron Leader Goddard arrived. He was a man of medium height, with black curly hair set well back on his forehead. I should say that he was about 36 years old. At his first church parade there was no electrical power in the drill hall, so we had to go into the recreation hall where he gave us a short talk instead of a sermon. He appealed to us not to let service life lower our standards.

'Don't try to keep up with the crowd by telling the best dirty story,' he said, 'Such practices were a betrayal of our families, sweethearts and wives at home. Try to keep up your characters.'

However, I doubt whether he had the confidence of the men and I do not think he would approve of the common practice in North America of telling dirty stories in mixed company.

According to a radio report Churchill had said that, during the month of May, 30 German submarines had been sunk in the Atlantic. It really did appear that we had now got the mastery of matters in the Atlantic.

On 13 July 1943 we had a sports day at No.38 SFTS. Both Ricky and I entered for a couple of events. I was in the tilt-the-bucket game, but came in nowhere. Mrs Lee Cox, the CO's wife, presented the prizes.

One June night the moon had no fewer than four rays radiating from it; this was something I had never seen before. The following day it was very hot and in the afternoon we had a thunderstorm. As the local farmers had, for some time now, been complaining about the lack of moisture, they should have been very happy.

For some time now, the meals in the airmen's dining room had improved. As an example, on 14th July the evening meal was delicious steak with gravy and potatoes, followed by stewed prunes. I had 15 prunes on my plate. Additionally, there were heaps of bread, bowls full of butter and jam, with two cakes for each man. This was pretty good going.

About this time we had a plague of four-winged dragonflies that got anywhere by the hundred; but since these insects live on mosquitoes, they were not altogether unacceptable.

28

By Train and Hitch-hiking to Los Angeles and Back

For some time Ricky and I had discussed the possibility that, on this year's two weeks annual leave, we should hitch-hike to Los Angeles. There were many difficulties about the idea. We needed to take our leave together and to get permission to visit the USA – for this was granted only when we could prove that an American was prepared to have us and to stand the expense of our stay. Canada would not allow Canadian currency to be taken into the USA. At work we were up against the decision of Flight Sergeant Fence, who ruled that he could only allow one man from each four man gang to be away at the same time. We now had to think out how we could get around some or all of these problems. Ricky got an American acquaintance of his at Crosby to write a letter of invitation to the States and he also got one for me, in the name of a man who had died six months previously. All this was necessary in order that the bank manager at Estevan might sign a form 'H' to send to the CO at Estevan airport. I happened to have an English friend named Jack Titley who was in the USA, working for Nestlé's chocolate firm, and about to join the US Army, so I wrote to him and he was quite obliging by sending me a letter inviting me to stay with him. He would also be willing to send me a money order in US currency to meet my expenses and I could eventually repay him by sending him a money order in Canadian currency.

As sometimes happens, the situation suddenly turned for the best, starting with Ricky's announcement that Sergeant Lucas had told him that we could both have leave together. This was soon followed by my receiving a reply from the Southern Pacific

Railway in Salt Lake City that they had received a deposit of some 30 dollars that I had sent to them for the purchase of a railway ticket to Los Angeles when I arrived in that city. You see, there was always the risk that either of us would lose our cash, or even have it stolen, and there would be nobody to whom we could turn to see us through with cash. Ricky had made all arrangements for his money and we were all right.

During the last few days before setting out, we polished our brass buttons and had our summer khaki uniform washed. At noon on Wednesday 21 July, armed with leave documents endorsed for a journey to the USA, we set out by taking a taxi from the guardroom to the border. When we arrived at the USA customs the keeper was digging his garden and stopped at it whilst his wife saw to us. We had no trouble at all and set off to walk on the first leg of our hitch-hike to Los Angeles. We started with a lift to Crosby and from there a farmer in a Montana rancher's truck that was loaded with cattle salt moved us 18 miles to Alamo and another car to Williston, where Ricky and I both picked up a small supply of US dollars that we had previously deposited with various people in the town. For the next bit of the journey, we decided to take the train that left the GNR station at 1.00 a.m. for Helena, a few hundred miles west, and following fairly closely the Canada/USA border. This train was called the 'Empire Builder' and we should travel in it all night to Helena in Montana. We had an evening meal in a Williston cafe and duly set out. When daylight broke I could see that the countryside was rather dry looking, with scattered dusty sage bushes on it. There were, of course, places where the land looked more fertile. The railway followed the general course of the Missouri river and at a place called Great Falls there was a large dam with a hydroelectric generating plant attached to it. In the train there was an American army policeman who told Ricky that it was not permitted to take any photos from the train.

During the early afternoon, as we approached Helena, the capital of Montana, there were some low hills parallel with the railway that were pock-marked with dark holes and there were spills of soil and rock below these holes. We afterwards found out that they were the long-disused remains of miners' excavations, where they had been prospecting for gold.

At 4.00 p.m. the train arrived in Helena, where we alighted and went into the town. We found a hotel where, after a wash and brush up, we went sightseeing. We were shown around the legislation buildings by an elderly caretaker. In the council chamber there was a large oil painting depicting the explorers Lewis and Clark meeting the Native American chiefs. We heard stories of around 1860 when quite large amounts of gold were found. About $30,000,000 worth of this placer, or free gold, was dug out. What was known as the Last Chance Gully is where the present main street now stands. We also heard that in the late 1860s there was a lot of trouble with lawless men who behaved like highwaymen. Many honest folk were shot dead for a few dollars. To combat this lawlessness, small groups of men known as vigilantes were formed to deal with the desperadoes and eventually they got the upper hand of them.

In a shop window, I was much taken by an oil painting that showed two Native Americans paddling their birch bark canoe up a stream of very clear water. I made up my mind that I would, if I had enough money as we came back, buy this painting. However, on our return journey there was not enough time to leave the station to get this picture.

Helena was a place were recruits were enlisted into the US army and the streets were littered with raw recruits; almost every one of them saluted Ricky and me. No doubt they had been told to salute all officers and were misled by seeing the two shoulder wings that all British airmen wore as signifying that we were qualified pilots. Ricky got tired of this saluting and said that we had better go back into our hotel to escape it.

On the next morning we turned our faces south in the direction of Salt Lake City and, more immediately, to the Yellowstone Park, famous for its hot water geysers. It was some time before we got a lift, but two highway officials named Zion and Devine speeded us in their car through what was now very interesting countryside. There were great rolling hills upon which stood several very large ranches. Wild antelopes were grazing within a quarter of a mile of the road.

At Three Forks, the Missouri River branches into three of its headwaters: the Jefferson, the Madison and the Gallatin. From there we did not do particularly well for rides, so when we did get to Gallatin Gateway we went into a cafe and had a drink of beer. Eventually a man called Taylor took us 35 miles to what was called No.320 Ranch. We passed through a very pretty valley lined with pine trees. Mr Taylor told us that he owned a ranch and holiday camp and that if we liked to do so we could stay the night there, for he had several empty holiday cabins. We agreed to do so, and soon we arrived at his ranch. About a dozen people were staying at this No.320 Ranch. We took our evening meal in the ranch house and soon chatted with the other people at table. Several people told us that they had been in the mountain streams panning for gold, although they had collected only a small amount of it. To them, it was part of their holiday fun to have a go and what little value the gold had did help to pay for their holiday.

We were told that across the highway and a little up the hill there was a colony of beavers, so after supper we decided to go and have a look at one of their dams. As we approached the dam we heard loud slaps as the fleshy flattened tails of the beavers slopped into the water: slap – slap – slap. All around the dam there were many young poplar trees, for the beavers lived by eating the bark of poplars. The animals had cut down many trees by biting through the bark of trunks about two feet from the ground. They then cut off pieces of the trunks in two foot long logs that they took into the water and buried them in the mud of the stream about three feet down to serve as their winter food when everything was frozen stiff. The dam was formed by dropping trees into the water and filling the holes up with small sticks and mud until the water was piled up like a mill dam. They then made a ledge under water, but piled up above water level and covered over with a mud roof, so that in winter they could live there safely under a wolf-proof roof of frozen mud and muck, as hard as iron. When they were hungry, all they had to do in winter was to fetch in one of the hidden logs of polar wood and eat the bark.

In the morning, after a breakfast of fried cut-throat trout, in the ranch house dining room where the walls were hung with skins of coyotes and the huge skull of a buffalo, we took to the road again. We soon got a lift by the local medical officer of health, who was collecting samples of drinking water. He put us down at West Yellowstone. We eventually found our way to the entrance to Yellowstone Park, where I particularly wanted to see the world famous hot geysers.

The keeper at the gatehouse refused to let us in on the grounds that we were hitch-hikers. A car came along, but the driver said that he was intending to go into the park in order to escape from mosquitoes. I had always wanted to see the geysers and I did not want to be put off and eventually the driver of the car said that he would take us in the park. At that, the gatekeeper, who had been told that Ricky and I had come all the way from Great Britain to see the geysers, promptly handed me a free entrance ticket with my name written on it. The car driver then said, 'Please be quick,' for the Old Faithful Geyser was some distance inside the park, and was due to 'blow up' in about ten minutes time – and it only blows up once every hour. We whizzed along beside the Firestone River for a few miles, and arrived just as the first puffs of steam and water were spurting up, with grumbles and burblings. Then the jet started to climb until it reached a height of about 150 feet, at which it remained for only about three minutes and then gradually subsided. The mechanics of this geyser are that at a great depth water flows into a crevice of rock that is at a high temperature, where superheated steam gradually builds up sufficient pressure to lift the water above it and give a spectacular display.

From the park we went down to West Yellowstone, where we hired a holiday bungalow and spent the evening at a dance. Sitting at the bar was a big burly man with whom we got chatting.

He asked us who we were, and then said, 'Well, chaps, I'm a logger in the woods all the week and on Saturday night I come here for a drink.' His wife came over, and he said to her, 'Here's three silver dollars,' and, handing them to her, he said, 'Give these boys a good time, but do not come bothering me.'

Two married couples whom we met at this social evening told us that they were leaving by car the next day and would be able to give us a lift for 100 miles on our way to Salt Lake City, so we agreed that we would willingly go with them. They gave us their address. The next day it was Sunday and we went to have our breakfast in a drug store. By my side at the long bar bench table was a middle-aged man who asked me who we were.

When I told him that we were British aircraftmen in the RAF, he seemed surprised and said, 'I thought that perhaps you were American Civil Defence men.' When I told him that we were making for Salt Lake City, he immediately said, 'I, too, am going there this afternoon. Can I give you a ride there in my car?'

When I told him that two other people had promised to give us a lift part of the way, he said that he was going there direct and would spin us down there in no time.

Ricky and I then set off to find the other folks, whom we found in a holiday cabin. They agreed to the change. We then went to an agreed meeting place with Maurice Yates, who was in his open Buick Eight model car, and he introduced his wife to us. He told us that he was a ranch owner and also a cattle dealer. To us this seemed an undreamed piece of luck and it was the longest bit of hitch-hiking in the whole trip. One thing that Maurice insisted upon was that he wanted to do a little more fishing.

When Ricky looked a bit doubtful about the extra delay, Maurice promptly said that, 'I travel fast and I guarantee that we shall be in Salt Lake City this evening.'

We certainly had to go back miles over the ground that we had travelled the previous day. We eventually came to the river where Maurice wanted to do a little more fishing, which was probably the Madison River. Getting out his fishing tackle and waist-high rubber wading boots, he started to cast, walking up and down the middle of the fast flowing river that was about a foot deep. Meanwhile, Ricky and I and Maurice's wife walked along the river bank, chatting pleasantly about this and that.

There were some rolling hills to the west of us and between us and them there was a wide expanse – almost square miles of it – that was covered with wild blue geraniums. From looking a bright blue near to us, the colour gradually faded down to a pale misty blue on the distant hillsides.

Maurice caught nothing, but he repeatedly said, 'I'll just have another run.'

His wife said nothing at all and showed no interest in the fishing, but at about 2.00 p.m. he decided to call it a day and we set off south at high speed. What a lovely ride that was, as we left the pine woods and hills of the Yellowstone plateau and were soon passing through the flattish grain and potato fields of eastern Idaho. Hereabouts there were large caves, known as frost-free cellars for the storage of potatoes in winter. The cave doors were large and wide enough for the tractors to enter with their loads. These cellars were large enough to hold hundreds of tons of potatoes in each of them. We stopped in one of the wayside small towns and had tea in a cosy little cafe and then pressed on along the road again. Maurice drove very fast. We found that he was a very well-educated gentleman and both he and his wife told us many interesting things as we went along.

At 10.30 p.m. we arrived at Salt Lake City, where Maurice dropped us at the United Services Club Hostel. This was a very smart and crowded place, with servicemen of all kinds being dealt with by very smartly dressed young women. In the middle of the main room there was a round table, with about half a dozen ladies dealing with all who cared to ask questions. One of these women said that her husband was in the US Army and now stationed at Huntingdon. She asked me to give her the names of a few saloons, pubs, in order that she might find out if he frequented them. We booked a room for the night.

Next morning we set out to have a look at the city and I must say that it looked very smart, clean and sun-washed, with some very beautiful buildings. I picked up the cash that I had posted to the Southern Pacific Railway, checked on the timetable and booked tickets for the next day's train to Los Angeles, before going out to see the city. There were cotton wood trees lining the streets of this city inhabited by 210,000 people. Everyone looked well-dressed and healthy and the sun was glorious. The city stands in a shallow hollow hemmed in on three sides by great dry-looking hills. On the western side there is the great salt lake, that glistens in the bright sunlight. We went up to the eastern side of the city, where stands the State Capitol building, to the grave of Brigham Young, the Mormon leader who, in 1847 brought pilgrims to Salt Lake City. We also visited the Mormon Gardens, where there were many lovely brightly coloured flower beds. We also went to the museum.

Hanging around were several well-dressed men who were obviously devotees of the Mormon religion. One of these gentlemen came up to me to ask who I was and where I had come from. He promptly replied that the next coming of Jesus Christ would be in America.

Looking at me with the light of conviction in his eyes, he said, 'I do hope that you will not return to Britain, because if you do so, you will be caught with your trousers down.'

Next day we got onto the Southern Pacific Railway's Challenger Express, that left at 10.20 a.m. en route for Los Angeles. As the train pulled out we had a splendid view of the Great Salt Lake across the western horizon. This lake is several miles wide and much longer than that. It was a sunny, hot day, but the coach was air-conditioned and quite cool.

Almost immediately after pulling out of Salt Lake City, we started to run over dry and arid looking soil and this would be more or less the case over the almost 700 miles of the Utah Desert. At first there were scanty patches of grass and bits of wiry sort of weed, as well a few stunted juniper trees. A hundred miles out there was little else but bare, parched ground, as the railway followed a wide, flat valley, with a background of distant jagged bare hills that presented an outline like that of a cross-cut saw. Never before had I seen a desert and this was a fascinating sight to me.

The train was hauled by a huge steam locomotive, a 4-8-2 two cylinder type, that seemed to press on regardless. At widely spaced places we stopped where there were track pits between the rails and men crept under the locomotive to oil its bearings. Others climbed onto the tender and filled up its water tank. It was very likely that the locomotive was an oil burner and if so the fuel tank would also be topped up. I am not sure how many miles the locomotive went west, but it may well have gone the whole way from Salt Lake City to Los Angeles.

At 2.00 a.m. next morning we got down from the train at Las Vegas in Nevada. We were not intending to spend time in the many gambling halls, but we wanted to see if there was a chance of getting to the Great Boulder Dam on the Colorado River. Although it was in the middle of the night, the first thing we saw in a park outside the station were several men, fully dressed, lying on their back fast asleep. Of course the night temperature was very high and permitted this outside sleeping. We soon found a hotel and booked, where we had a very comfortable night.

Las Vegas is a very small town, right in the middle of desert country and not far from the dreadful Death Valley, which is below sea level and very torrid. This place is about five miles westwards. In Las Vegas there are two exhibited examples of the four-wheeled wagons that in earlier days were used to bring out borax, hauled by teams of 15 mules. Death Valley is now a national park.

Between 9.00 and 10.00 a.m. we walked on to the road that led east some 20 or 30 miles to the Great Boulder Dam. Our luck was in, because almost immediately a car drew up with a middle-aged couple in it called Slim and Gussey, who had only got married two months previously. They offered us a ride and as soon as they knew that we were British and trying to get to the Boulder Dam, they immediately said that they, too, would go there. The route passed through very arid land upon which only a few shrubs could grow. Littered about, at the rate of about one every surrounding couple of acres, were small amounts of large stones. We were told that the area was reputedly rich in minerals and that these piles of six or seven stones marked claims made by various prospectors and were still valid. Already a magnesium extracting plant had been built in the area, and put into operation. It certainly looked as if that vast area was practically loaded with various valuable metals.

At the Boulder Dam the road crossed the top of the dam, with the Colorado River some 800 feet below, deep down in the great rift of the valley. As it was wartime, a US Army guard was in place, every car was accompanied across the dam and we, too, had to get onto an army vehicle in a convoy of vehicles headed by an armoured car that had a swivel-mounted automatic gun pointing back at us. Looking down, we could just see the thin dark line of the river so deeply below. This was a most impressive sight, and I would not have missed it for anything.

We spent the rest of the day with Slim and Gussey in Las Vegas. These very kind people would insist on buying presents for ourselves and for our wives. We wandered around several of the gambling saloons and bars. I had a go at a gambling machine and to my utter surprise I won the jackpot of $4.00.

One of the chaps in the bar came up to me and said, 'I guess that you are a stranger here – you now have to treat everybody in the bar to a drink,' and I did so with pleasure.

That evening we took a night train to Los Angeles. During the night the land altitude began to lift as we approached the foothills of the California mountains. At daylight we could see that the mountains were quite high, ochre coloured and with tall Joshua pine trees growing the deep and shady valleys; they had a palm-like appearance with their tufts of leaves sticking from their tops. Very soon we began to descend to the Pacific coast. It was not long before groves of oranges appeared on the lineside, and at 2.00 p.m. we pulled in to Los Angeles. What a lovely railway station it was – it even had a colourful garden outside. We reported to the United Services Organisation's office on the station and they immediately told us that they were passing us on to the Hollywood Guild at Hollywood, some eight miles away. When we arrived we were given a warm welcome and a light meal, before being shown our sleeping place in a converted garage, where it was so warm all through the night that we never had to close the doors. The whole place was just marvellous and everything was free whilst we stayed there. The lady hostesses were most helpful in every way and they were beautifully dressed.

Ricky and I soon went out into the surrounding town, where it was something for us to see orange trees with lots of oranges on them as they grew alongside the pavements. We at once, when nobody was looking, picked a couple of oranges apiece. The following day we hitch-hiked six miles to Santa Monica beach and whilst we were looking for a place where we could change into bathing suits for a bathe in the sea, a lady with whom we chanced to speak, willingly let us go into her house to do so. The sea was very warm, with five foot high rollers pounding in from the Pacific. After that we decided to have a swordfish supper, and the waitress told us that the fish had been caught near Catalina island. It was a lovely meal, costing just $1.25. After that we took a bus ride to the Hollywood Canteen, where a stage show was put on for the benefit of military men. Hedy Lamarr a popular screen actress of the day, came onto the stage dressed in a red velvet gown, with two red bows in her black hair. Mickey Rooney, a popular drummer of the time, also gave a short performance.

On the following day, Saturday, we called on some people whose address had been given to Ricky by an airman friend at Estevan. They were most friendly folks, of middle-age, and they straight away took us in their car on a tour of Los Angeles and Hollywood. We saw a pond of natural gas and went into the Farmer's Market, where we had a barbecued tea sitting under a sun shade that was brightened by a very colourful pattern. We sat there for some time, watching the passers-by, and our talk was about England, the USA and Australia. Like many other Americans, we were told by these new friends how much they admired English law and justice. As it grew dark we went to the Planetarium, where we saw the stars and planets projected on the inside of the immense dome, and supported by an hour's lecture afterwards. What a lovely day we did have with these most friendly people.

Although we had seen far more of California than we had expected, on Sunday we got a little greedy by setting out on a trip south to San Diego, that was 150 miles away, and close to the Mexican border. We tried very hard to get lifts, but they came few and far between. Actually, there was plenty of traffic, but we did not get more than a ride of about 20 miles with a party of black members of a baseball team, who took us to a little place on the coast called Newport. Most of the country over which we travelled was yellowish in colour and given over to groves of orange trees, avocado pears and walnuts, all growing under irrigation. We turned back in the late afternoon and at Laguna Beach we had a bathe in the sea before setting off home to Los Angeles.

A US Army Air Corps captain gave us a lift. He said that if we came to Long Bush Airport in the morning, he would see if he could get us a lift in a bomber plane back to Great Falls. Monday 2 August was our last day in Los Angeles. We took a bus to Long Bush Airport, passing on the way through one of the oil-bearing districts, where the nodding arms of the oil-pumping derricks were as thick as the trees in a wood. At the airfield we were questioned by the military police, who eventually put identification discs on our tunics. We found Captain Del Monte, who told us that the next plane to Great Falls would be on Wednesday, so we decided to go back by train, lest there should be further hold-ups. A gasoline tanker driver gave us a lift back into Los Angeles.

This fattish man told us that he had no love of the Jews, saying: 'We must get rid of those sons of bitches.'

That evening we got on a train bound for Salt Lake City. When it stopped for 15 minutes at one of the inspection points, Ricky and I got down for a coffee and some cherry pie. It was a 24 hours journey to Salt Lake City, but when we got there we had a little discussion outside the station and decided to go on another 27 miles to a place called Ogden. We did so and stayed the night there. In the morning we set out north quite early, with the intention of getting to Butte. Rides, however, were not very easy. Two old ladies took us, very slowly, for a few miles, whilst a man on his way to repair a corn binder took us three miles and a highways official another two miles, and for the next 30 miles we rode in a sheep truck. It was a similar situation right up to Idaho Falls. Mind you, the country through which we passed was very pretty, and we passed large orchards of peaches and apricots. I bought for ten cents, 5p, three pounds of delicious apricots.

At Idaho Falls we saw a cowboy rodeo in which there was a bull riding display. We passed through a small town the name of which was, I think, Bozeman, where Ricky said that, after the war, he would like to come out and settle. Whether or not he actually did so, I never knew. After our slow progress that particular day we decided to take the train to Helena, and we spent the night in the train. At first the railway passed through mountainous country where the hillsides were pocked with dark little holes left by prospecting miners many years ago. As we left the train at Helena two girls gave us books, cigarettes and chocolate. In the town I bought, for a dollar, a pocket knife that I kept and used until the time that I began to write up a summary of my diary in 1996. After all those years, I think that this knife fell off the dresser and fell into the waste paper basket.

On the Wednesday we caught the morning train, 'Empire Builder', of the GN Railway, to travel back to Williston, where we arrived next day at 7.00 p.m., dirty, unshaven and hungry – we were also very tired. We went straight to the GN Hotel, booked a room for the night, and had a good wash, shaved and changed our clothes. In the morning we had a good breakfast of fried eggs, before setting out again to the north. Rides came very scantily and at Stady we sat on the grass beside a large prairie slough for two and three quarter hours. At long last we did get a lift with a farmer, who almost immediately told us that the previous week there had been a bad air accident at Estevan SFTS, in which several men had been killed. We were riding in a truck that had been used to cart pigs, and I must say that it smelt badly of pigs. Two Norwegian ladies picked us up for our next ride, taking us right up to the border post. From there we called a taxi to take us to the airfield. Our long trip was over, but what a marvellous journey it had been. Reckoning up, we decided that we had travelled around 4,000 miles, with 1,000 miles hitch-hiking and 3,000 miles by train. Train fares had cost us some $42.00 and altogether I had spent $90.00, or about £33.00 in English money.

Very soon after we got back into the SFTS we heard details of the air crash. It seems that Pilot Officer Bancroft, the man who had split the covering of the wing skins and probably the main spars of Anson 8583 in which I was flying earlier in the year, had been killed. The others killed were Flight Sergeant Lucas, fitters Tom Sayers and Cox, and electrician Riley. It seems that the plane had hit the ground, doubtless during low flying and nothing more was heard about it all. Of course, both Ricky and I knew each of the killed men, for they worked in our hangar.

29

Back to the Work of Winning the War

When I went back to work, there was not a lot of work to do in the hangar. We did have to start an inspection on the starboard engine of No. 8503, but it did appear to be in fairly good condition. Jock Smith, our fitter in charge, had been made a corporal at last. When I had to have some dental attention, I found that the dentist seemed in a hurry, and used a coarse drill as if he was drilling cast iron.

We finished the work on No. 8503, but when Sergeant Hall came round he carried out an inspection. He found a loose cowling bolt and noticed that the crankcase breather pipe was likely to chafe on a copper pipe that carried oil at pressure. I had to put both jobs right. One afternoon I had to attend a lecture on nuts and bolts and speed on a Stirling. A few days later I had to attend another lecture on valve timing of the Jacob's engines, so you see we had plenty of official instructions on how to do our work. We even had a lecture on supercharging, although none of our engines had superchargers. One day Sergeant Woodcock told us that on a grindstone a low carbon steel gives off a bright red spark and that higher carbon steels give off a duller red spark, whilst a high speed steel gives a bursting spark.

A new barrack officer named Judd, who had recently been given a commission, introduced a domestic night. Each space had to be washed down, and I was given the job of washing two doors. When PO Judd came round at 7.00 p.m., he told Corporal Forstead that the urinal trough was badly corroded, and that it was an easy task for an airman to remove this stain with an old razor blade. I could see more trouble to come.

At work on No. 8572 things started to go wrong. One of the engine bearer bolts stuck fast, and Sergeant Hilliard had a look at it and said he thought it would be all right. For myself, it seemed best to put the matter right and, helped by Corporal 'Lofty' Crawford, we tried to get the bolt out, but the result was that we cross-threaded it. All that we could do was to start again next morning, and lift the engine out to get a new bolt in place. Our old room mate 'Taffy' had just arrived back after 21 days' detention in the military barracks at Winnipeg.

24 August 1943 I flew with No. 8572 on a test flight. The pilot, a fat little young man, at first seemed very bad-tempered. He grumbled because the electrician was not there, before he had a go at me because I had left the pilot's seat in order to put my parachute harness on whilst he was away in No. 1 Hangar. He said that the machine might have moved off. When we got into the air, I was in the pilot's seat and he was in the co-pilot's seat, he snapped at me telling me to keep my feet off the rudder controls. We flew west over the prairie that looked up at us in yellow and brown with all the harvest work showing up below us. Everything went well with the plane and it was a lovely morning to be up in the air. A distant bank of clouds over the eastern horizon had sunlit tops that gave them the appearance of snow-capped mountains.

The commanding officer inspected our barracks on the morning of 24 August. He found several things that he did not like and a few new orders came out. All webbing equipment must be removed from the bed frames, two blankets must be placed over the ends of each bed, all shoes were to be kept clean and no pictures were allowed on the walls, neither were there to be any shades on the lamps.

Most of Friday 27 August I spent by being examined by the Central Canada Trade Test Board, who were here to see if there were too many leading aircraftsmen, with a view to weeding out many whose knowledge was not up to standard. I was lucky, in that one of the members of the test board had been taken ill with appendicitis at Waybourne SFTS, I was examined by my own Sergeant Hilliard for 50 minutes. I felt afterwards that I had come out reasonably well on all but precision instruments. In the afternoon I was examined on basic matters, this time by a squadron leader, who asked me to describe how I would set about cutting a keyway in a round metal shaft. He told me that my idea would not work. A few days afterwards Sergeant Hall told me that only about 44% passed the board test.

Corporal Oldbury said that he was about to marry the daughter of a local homesteader. This man had already been quite near to marrying other girls, but he seemed more likely to make a go of this affair. Corporal Napper, Oldbury's friend, said that Oldbury was a silly young boy who thought that he was marrying into money, but Darkie said that he was going to marry trouble.

It was domestic day in the billets, so I had to hand-scrub all the lavatory bowls. This was a most distasteful job, if you like, for the bowls were filthed up – some chaps treat the lavatory bowls in a dreadful way.

30

Progress of the War, Late 1943

There continued to be an improvement in the progress of the war. The latest news was that the British Eighth Army had taken Catania in Sicily and that the Russians were pushing ahead and had taken Orel.

Information from Germany reported a reorganization of the army; the high command had been transferred from Hitler to military experts. United States forces had captured the Japanese air base at Munda in the South Pacific, so things were much better than they were a year ago.

In August 1943, Winston Churchill arrived in Canada for a conference with President Roosevelt in Quebec. Some people speculated that this visit to Canada might have portended coming action by Canadian troops, who might be used to invade Germany. Whilst in the United States earlier that year, I could not help noticing how the American girls and women were changing over to the wearing of trousers. In Los Angeles I saw that many women, not content with wearing the trousers full length, had already started to turn them up above their knees. This was something new that came out of the war. In America, of course, clothing was more readily obtainable than in Britain.

Over the radio we heard that the campaign in Sicily was nearing its end, for the Axis troops were penned up in the northeast corner near Messina. I wondered how many of these Germans would manage to escape by crossing the narrow sea over to Italy, or whether we should take most of them prisoners. From the Far East came news that the Japanese had abandoned Kiska in the Aleutians. From England I learned that a March farmer had been fined £15.00 for driving his car to Peterborough on unauthorized petrol. A Peterborough civilian was found not guilty of the manslaughter of a Whittlesy fellow during a drunken brawl with some American soldiers.

Winston Churchill, speaking from Quebec on 31 August said that although he had hoped that he would be able to announce peace with Italy, this was not yet possible, but that some day British and American troops would be able to sail across the English Channel to invade France. Political considerations would not rush us into a premature attack. British bombers had again raided Berlin, with the loss of 48 planes, and it seemed to me that we could scarcely maintain replacements of so many machines.

It was a big day in the war when Italy made an unconditional surrender to the Allies, as happened on 8 September 1943, Churchill, who seemed obliged to promise something about a second front, had said that an invasion force was ready to strike across the Channel against the Germans in Europe. The time and day were still secret.

Anthony Eden, the British foreign secretary, had said in the House of Commons that Rudolph Hess came from Germany two years ago with peace plans. Generally speaking, they appeared to have been based on the maintenance of the British Empire and some Russian territory for Germany and the return of her old colonies. These details had been kept secret for two years.

George Marshall, an American general, has been appointed commander-in-chief of all Allied forces. To me, it does seem as if the majority of commands have been given to Americans and others agree with me. All that we can hope is that these men prove capable leaders.

On the radio news that morning, 4 September, it was announced that the British Eighth Army had firmly established itself on the toe of Italy and was moving north and east. A few days later, the news came through that the Eighth Army had entrenched themselves on the Italian coast. To me it seemed that, although we were making progress, the Germans were bound to put up a long and protracted fight to hold us back in Italy. It was still a long way to the Brenner Pass.

All radio reports 16 September told us of very fierce fighting at

Salerno, near Naples, where the US Army was attempting to force an inland thrust from a 25 mile sea front. The Germans appeared well-positioned in the hills, from which they rained down a murderous fire on our men on the beaches. Bernard Montgomery's British Eighth Army was racing against time along the coast to join in the battle; that day they were still 35 miles away. Fortunately, the next day's news told us that the Eighth Army had made contact with the Americans in front of Salerno.

According to a newspaper report, Churchill proposed to call a conference of all British Empire countries, and even suggested an Empire cabinet. At least it appeared that, at long last, the British were going to look after their Empire. Some day, too, Canada would be a great country. Churchill had also just told a conference of English women that the war effort must be kept at full swing for another two years. He was sure that by that time Germany will be beaten.

31

Farms and Countryside

In response to a request made through the YMCA for volunteers to give farmers a hand at harvest time, several chaps spent their 48 hours weekend leave working on farms. The work given to them was usually stooking corn or helping with the threshing. They were paid about $5.00 a day, and they were fed and kept by the farmer – but more about this later.

After tea one day I went down to the Long Creek River, where I found some choke cherries almost ripe and not bad to eat. As I came back I startled up a fully grown reddish brown deer that had a longish, upright white tail. Finding a deer so close to the airfield rather surprised me, but about five minutes later I was even more surprised when two splendid fawns jumped out of some low bushes and bounded away.

The weather during early August was fine and very pleasant. Day after day we had lovely sunshine and I felt that this was a wonderful country. I was sure that when I returned to Britain I should miss all this splendid weather. Out here we never thought of the need to take a raincoat.

On Saturday 28 August I set out to visit some French farming people by the name of Gervais, for I had met one of the sons named Herman and promised to come over and give them a day's help with their harvest, at a place called Hitchcock. Flight Lieutenant Engleston, our medical officer, picked me up and dropped me near Hitchcock, where the elevator foreman pointed out that the Gervais farm lay about three miles across the prairie to the north-east. I walked it and found old Mrs Gervais washing clothes in the back yard. Herman was helping a German neighbour named Nasie Schnell to thresh barley. I gave them a hand for half an hour in the field where they had a motor tractor driving a threshing machine in the middle of a field.

The Gervais farm was, as usual, dominated by a large wooden barn, painted red, and with horses, pigs and so on on the ground and hay in the loft. The house was clean and tidy, with the old folks sleeping on the ground floor living room. One of their sons was in the army, whilst one or two girls were away school teaching. The upstairs room was divided by a large screen made of sacking that separated the boys from the girls. That night Herman and myself shared what was normally the girls' part of the bedroom and the main covering was a large overall cover that was well sprinkled with barley horns after having served as a sheet to block holes in one of the barley harvesting wagons. The old folks spoke better French than English. Herman was about 18 and a very pleasant lad whose appearance was spoilt by a decayed front tooth.

On the following day, Sunday, Herman, Gerard, Fred, a friend, and myself set about stooking a 90 acre field of oats. In this field there were many scratchings made by badgers digging for gophers which they eat. In another field that lay as rough grazing land near the house I saw many smallish holes of about 2 inches diameter and was told that these were inhabited by small owls. I never found out whether these birds remained for the winter in Canada, although I felt that they were migrants.

The Schnells had a largish horse pond in which I had a bathe. At the end of the day I think that there was a bit of an argument about who should pay me for my share of the work, but in the end I was paid about five or six dollars.

Wherever I went, the farmers always wanted to tell me how drought during the years 1929 to 1939 plagued them. Old farmers told how it was often necessary to pay $20 a ton for hay, which they then had to cart 20 or 30 miles from the nearest railroad, for feeding their cattle and horses. Everywhere the fields stood dry and bare, dust blew everywhere and everybody wondered when the climate would change.

When I mentioned to farmers that probably there was a need for irrigation, they did not agree with me, considering that this would not be practicable.

About mid-September I noticed that there had been a gathering of large flocks of blackbirds. Thousands of them thronged the fields, so when I saw a farmer shovelling wheat into an outhouse I asked him the reason for this congregation of birds. He said that they had been doing this for several days, and it meant 'bad weather'. Personally, I still felt that the birds were about to migrate for the winter, but in the event a heavy fall of unwelcome rain came, supporting the farmer's prediction.

About this time I made a hitch-hiking trip to a little prairie town called Arcola, which was about 30 miles east of Estevan Like most of these small places, the wide earthen street was set at right angles to the railroad and at the end of the street there was the invariable hotel beside the railroad track. There were duckboards along the sidewalks in front of the leaning and dilapidated wooden stores and one of two cafes. Foremost among the buildings were the garages, which were also the registered agencies for the big farm implement makers such as Massey Harris, McCormick, Deering and so on. There were also hardware stores selling farm tools and household necessities. There were several brick buildings that leaned inwards or outwards, the result of work by unskilled bricklayers. The largish hotel had few visitors. About 10 years ago the population was 1,500 but today it is down to 500 people. Such is the picture of many prairie small towns.

The aurora borealis, or northern lights, are seen but rarely in the British Isles, but whilst I was in Canada they appeared several times. In September 1943 there was a good show of them in the night sky. There was a broad arc of dark cloud that was lit up by shafts of moving light radiating upwards against it across the northern sky.

Canadian local government was something that I never knew much about. According to Ricky Rickard there was a small clique of business men who tried to run the town of Estevan to their own advantage. The bus owner seems to be a rather officious sort of chap. It was said that he tried to stop the camp motor transport giving rides to airmen into town because this took away some of his bus trade.

I had recently stayed the night in a little wooden hotel at a place called Qu'Appelle. They say that this place takes its name from the language of the French Canadian half-breed Native Americans and means 'Who calls?', as the Native American name in the musical *Rose Marie*. I went the 14 miles north to Fort Qu'Appelle, where there was a post of the Hudson's Bay Company. Mr Hudson, the town clerk, showed me the little log cabin which was all that remained of the old post. Here was the mile-wide valley of the Qu'Appelle River and a large irrigation lake upstream. I was shown the skull of a Native American that had been dug up – it had beautifully sound teeth, owing, perhaps, to chewing old bones. Here was also much bush country; all poplar trees were now loaded with golden leaves. Much grain was grown between the clumps of bushes. The hitch-hiking was hard going, for I did not see a car between 3.00 p.m. and 5.00 p.m.

32

Work, Deserters and Crime

On the first day of April a new regulation was brought into force when airmen were using the dining hall. From now on only dining hall cutlery was to be used at meals, no longer could individuals use their own cutlery or drinking mugs. The washing-up of all dining room dirty knives, forks, spoons and other items was to be done in the washing-up machine. Admittedly the standard of washing up had fallen off badly; often enough one found half the last man's meal sticking on his plate. I decided that I would wait until there were no knives or other cutlery, I would then revert to my former custom of taking my own.

I went to the next church parade, at which the commanding officer told an under-flying-instruction pilot to have his sideboards cut off. The padre had introduced a piano and we had a small orchestra of four players. In his sermon he said that freedom was not to do just as one pleased, but to act in some way ordered towards a right purpose. He proposed to dedicate next Sunday's service to special prayers for wives at home.

Three high-spirited young airmen, MacArdie, Noolan and Stevenson, were detained in the 'cooler' for having stolen somebody's car in Estevan. An airman named Thomas, a general duties man who used to work in the cookhouse as a washer-up, has been taken to Regina on a charge of rape against a young local girl of 14.

Some of the airmen discovered that by buying liquid tea at the YMCA cheaply by the gallon they could resell this at the tea breaks in the hangars at about 3 cents a cup and make a nice profit. So many fellows took advantage of this arrangement that the mobile YMCA tea wagon had very few customers. The YMCA stopped the practice, so then there were the old long lines of men waiting in the queue for drinks.

Another wave of crime seemed to be sweeping across the station. A Welshman named Thomas, who had previously been mentioned as being mixed up in a rape case, had been sentenced to three years' imprisonment by the Royal Canadian Mounted Police. Further, a flight mechanic named Collins, a prominent athlete and a man of the world, accompanied by another airman named Ballinger, stole a car at a dance in Lampman and took off the wheels and tyres, for rubber is valuable. The sum of $100,000 had also been stolen from the station YMCA.

Strangely enough, a Bible was asked for in our barrack room recently. One man only, a chap named Woody, had a Bible with him. What somebody wanted to know was how many wives David had and how he was always begetting children by some woman or other.

The custom of flying with planes on test flights continued, and I happened to be on plane 8527 with Sergeant Cutler. Sergeant Hart and a rigger flew with us and one of them was in the co-pilot's seat as we lifted up into a dullish morning with very high cloud. I was standing up behind the pilot watching the revolution counters of the engines when the plane was suddenly lifted up into a steep climb, so sudden that I fell over. That's the result of flying with other people who take the seats. After landing, our gang was given the afternoon off, but this was spoilt by having to report for rifle practice. It was the first time that I had fired a rifle since leaving Halton Training Camp two years previously.

Bobby Lane, a little chap who worked on engines in the hangar, went to the tool store one day, where he became involved in an argument with the storekeeper; words followed, and he was put on a charge for cheek to an NCO. Then he had to do five days on 'jankers'.

It was noticeable at Estevan how much a higher standard of discipline was enforced upon under-training pilots than upon the general ground staff. Pupils were marched in orderly fashion, they had to salute smartly every officer. The chaps in our hangar said that any old mechanic could go into the flight commander's office without saluting, but no pupil dared do it. Actually, in our hangar we were expected to salute officers, even when wearing overalls. I hated doing this, because it seemed unreasonable.

Sometimes we engine fitters had a deuce of a job with the engines on a plane. A typical example occurred when we had Anson 8435, when the fuel gauges on both engines registered low pressure. The port engine responded to an adjustment of the pump relief valve.

As the starboard engine still showed a fluctuation of petrol pressure, Sergeant Hillard said, 'Change the pump', but the fuel pump was in a very awkward position to get it out, situated as it was between the magneto, dynamo, oil pump and the self-starter.

We put a new pump on, but there were still the same old fluctuations. We next pulled off the petrol pipe from the tank, proved that there was a clear flow of petrol up to the tank selector cocks, but still no joy. We then removed the entire selector cock assembly, but found that it was quite clear. We next tried running the engines on the starboard tanks, but the whole petrol supply failed and both engines stopped dead. Sergeant Hillard then had the thought that there might be an air leak somewhere, so next day we had to fit a new selector cock. And that is how things used to go.

In addition to the repair of engines, there were also extra duties for us, such as duty crash gang, or the fire piquet. The crash gang had to go to meals early, and return to work in the hangar for the purpose of helping to push in machines for the night. Whilst on fire piquet we had to attend a lecture from 7.00 to 8.00 p.m. on how to use fire extinguishers, and whilst this was in progress one evening we had to turn out to a crash landing of 8565 which had come down in the dark with the undercarriage in the up position. We used a motor-powered crane to lift up the machine and bring it into a hangar. It was around 10.00 p.m. when we got finished and as we walked back to our barrack room there was seen, away in the west, a two mile long prairie fire blazing brightly.

In early September 1943 one of our airframe fitters named Morrell who had been missing as a deserter for some time, was brought back to Estevan. It was said that he had sold all his RAF uniform, dressed himself in civvy clothes, obtained a job as a taxi driver and found himself a lady friend in Regina. He apparently had fallen out with this lady and she had given him away to the police or RAF authorities. It was also said that the same thing had happened with two other chaps who had deserted and gone into the United States and had also been given away by women who had spilled the beans on them.

A hangar notice was posted 5 October 1943 saying that we must work harder and that unless we did so, 48 hour leave passes would have to be curtailed.

The results of the Central Canada Trade Test Board came out – I had passed at 82.6%.

Each man had to see Pilot Officer Lewis, the technical adjutant, and I failed to salute him, so he said, 'Bonnett, when I go into the CTO's office I salute him and it might be as well if you did the same when you come in here.'

I said, 'Sorry, sir,' and gave him a salute, although I was dressed in dirty overalls.

One day I went to dinner without my cap and a special police officer standing inside the dining hall yelled out at me, 'Airman, where is your cap?' All that I could say was that I had left it in my room. He immediately said, 'Report to the station warrant officer at 6.00 p.m.'

I did so, and was told to clean up one bowl in the officers' lavatory, for this SWO was a decent old sort, who never dished out heavy punishments.

About this time I had to report to the dental officer for some attention to my teeth. I had a heavily stopped tooth which the army officer dentist did not seem keen to remove.

He had an awful job trying to move the tooth, and all he could say was, 'My goodness, I would not like to pull a mouthful of these bastards out every day.'

He did get the tooth out, but only after splitting it into several pieces. I think this tooth came out in about 30 pieces and the last bit about a year later.

Canadian Pacific locomotive of the 2-10-4 wheel arrangement is shown here on public view at Windsor Station in Montreal in 1931. (Canadian Pacific Railway Archives No. 22136)

Four aircraftmen from 38 SFTS Estevan in Regina Street in March 1943. From left to right: Alan Vinall, Harry Williams, Bert Marshall and Harold Bonnett.

The author pushing the wheel-barrow in the 1943 tilt the bucket race at the Sports Day of 38 SFTS at Estevan.

The author sitting in a boat during the 1943 flooding of the Souris River between Estevan town and the airfield.

A 1943 scene with the author sitting in the seat of a lightweight four wheel gig that had been home-made by a Ukranian settler. The location was the horse and cart park in Estevan.

A hitch hiking ride in 1943 with the author standing on top of the second tender of a Canadian Pacific locomotive as it passed along the foot of the Rockies.

Ricky Rickard and the author outside the log cabin that we hired for one night at No. 320 ranch 1943 near Yellowstone, USA. Between the elk antlers there was the skull of a buffalo.

Maurice Yates, his wife and Ricky in the Yates's car before we set off on the Sunday afternoon run of some 360 miles from Yellowstone to Salt Lake City.

The author on the parcel of land that he bought at Cowichan Lake on Vancouver Island in 1943. The Cowichan River is behind me.

A 1944 view looking west up the Alaska Highway at a point about a hundred miles north of its commencement. It was a very cold place up there in winter.

Author skating in 1942 on an Estevan prairie slough or pond in November. The dog "Jankers' was the mascot of No.38 SFTS at Estevan. Some chaps said that this dog came over on the boat with us when we came from Britain.

A 1943 photo of an Anson I Aircraft on the concrete forecourt at No.38 SFTS Estevan. These planes were powered by seven cylinder radial engines made by the Jacobs Company, Pottstown, Pennsylvania USA.

33

Events at the End of 1943

Taffy who lived in our barrack room, was once more on a charge, this time for not being on church parade. When two fellows answered his name at roll call, one said, 'Sick', and the other, 'On leave.' So he had to see the CO.

Supper was served in the dining hall at 8.30 p.m. and sometimes there was some tasty tea to drink. One evening I sat with Joe Knightly, who hailed from Boston, Lincolnshire, and we chatted about steam ploughing and the possibility of making a model steam plough engine. He suggested oscillating cylinders, but I hardly agreed with that.

During a conversation with a Canadian sailor, and I don't know where this happened, he described his experiences of an encounter with German submarines in the Atlantic. According to him, the German submarines surfaced and fought it out with escorting warships. The German sailors seemed fearless, pressed home their attacks with gunfire, and they had already sunk several of our ships that way. I think that the Germans had got a little tired of being submerged, where they were quickly detected and blown to pieces with depth charges.

Flight Sergeant Penny told me that if I had a little more seniority I might have been recommended for promotion to corporal.

There had been a little trouble in No. 7 hangar. Several chaps due to go on leave for 48 hours had been refused permission to go at noon one Friday. Flight Lieutenant Zielony, the officer in charge, definitely refused early finishing for all, except those who were expecting to travel by train.

When one chap said that he was travelling by car to Regina, he said, 'Well, in that case your friends can quite easily call for you after 5.00 p.m.'

Bert Marshall, who was in our room, told Ricky that a few years ago he had courted a girl in England. They planned marriage and, since he had no bank account, he had paid his spare cash to his bride to be. When he had paid some £300 that way, she jilted him in order to marry another chap. Bert was then courting a Norwegian girl who lived in the USA.

The war news was that the Russians had made further advances against the Germans in south Russia. According to the papers there was a good possibility that many Germans might have been trapped and taken prisoner. However, they were not fools at war business and I expected many would have escaped being surrounded.

In the Regina paper, there was an account of how a Calgary hunter was badly mauled by a female grizzly bear in the Rockies. After wounding the bear with three rifle bullets, it charged him and it was only by feigning death that he managed to survive. The bear had two cubs with it and, since they may have been about seven months old at the time, if their mother had died of gunshot wounds they may have survived, but this was doubtful.

A new order had come out saying that airmen must sleep with their heads at opposite ends – i.e. those in the bottom beds must sleep with their heads next to the gangway, whilst those above must sleep with their heads against the wall. The powers that be said that this arrangement lessened the liability of breathing one another's breath, with a smaller risk of spreading colds, etc. To me it seemed that sleeping as we did 20 in a room with all the windows sealed in winter, it did not matter much whether we slept this way or that.

One very sunny late October day I happened to be travelling in a train that stopped at Weyburn. I noticed that there were three rats swimming around in a bare and very dirty pond by the railway side. They would swim for a few feet, suddenly quicken their pace and dive under the water, where they remained for about a minute. Whatever in the way of food these rats found below in the dirty water, I did not know, but they did not look like water rats. Perhaps they were muskrats?

Mr Churchill had spoken in London at the Lord Mayor's Show. He said that Hitler still had 400 Divisions in the field and an early peace was not to be expected. We must, during 1944, expect that there would be great battles, with heavy losses of life for both British and American forces. He went on to give great credit to the Russians for what he called the most outstanding achievement of 1943, for they had expelled the Germans from two thirds of occupied Russia.

On 10 November a large formation of wild duck flew over in a V-shaped formation at 5.00 p.m. heading south on migration. It seemed as if the snowfalls of the last few days must have reminded them that it was time they left Canada for the less cold south.

I had already enquired about the possibility of my getting a commission and I was interviewed by Wing Commander Ihrens. He read out the main things that I should know and it did not appear likely that I would get a commission. What he did say was that he admired my remustering to a fitter whilst in Canada.

'I do like to hear of people who do something off their own bat.'

However, he would see if I could qualify for a commission in motor transport or in general duties.

We were told that a new system would be introduced for major repairs on engines. Each gang would comprise five men, who would have to complete a machine's two engines in five days, or in the same time as allowed for the riggers. A new gang, to be known as the general gang would run up the engines after these repairs and also help when cylinders required heavy servicing. There was always something new like this, which seemed to be aimed at getting more work done.

Regarding my prospects for getting a commission, I was given a medical examination, but as it looked as if I should not qualify for anything much, other than a mechanical transport officer, I went over to the motor transport side at Estevan, but the NCO in charge soon told me that he did not want his men wasting time showing me the ins and outs of motor transport. This sort of remark put me off, and I felt that I should get nowhere with getting a commission. Although I did get sent to Winnipeg for an interview, I did not hear anything further for a long time and gave up the quest.

One late November afternoon I went down to the river creek for some skating. Four under-training pilots also arrived and we gathered a few dry sticks and made a fire on an exposed sand bar in the middle of the river. The gentle heat from this bonfire was most welcome. I was advised not to volunteer for pilot training. All the prospective pilots told me that they were browned off with the continual study.

Early in December 1943, whilst one of our aircraft was taking off, piloted by a pupil who was flying on instruments only, it veered off the runway and crashed into two machines parked in front of the control tower. Each of the machines involved was badly damaged.

34

My Last Weeks at No. 38 SFTS Eskevan

On Wednesday 15 December 1943 we all had to assemble in the drill hall, where visiting Air Vice-Marshal T.E. Lawrence told us that No. 38 SFTS unit was to be repatriated.

'It will not happen for a month,' he said, although plans were being laid to return us all as soon as possible.

This was great news, and most chaps were pleased. Corporal 'Ginger' Whitacker, who was expecting shortly to marry an American girl, was not pleased; he wanted to stay in Canada.

One afternoon I flew with Wing Commander H. J. Ihrens in 8520 on a test flight. The ground temperature was 5 degrees centigrade, but at 2,000 feet it was 10C. We flew over the frontier and circled the two custom buildings before going back over the town of Estevan. The wing commander did not recognize me in my working blue and parachute harness, and said, 'I did not recognize you, Bonnett.'

The MO confined all personnel to camp on account of a 'flu epidemic. At the cinema only alternate seats could be occupied. It was said that these restrictions were due to a rather mild winter that led to the 'flu epidemic.

My father, William Bonnett died 16 December 1943, aged 81 years, but it was not until 13 January that I received notice of this, due to the general hold up of trans-Atlantic postal services for war reasons. According to the radio news, Winston Churchill, who was suffering from pneumonia somewhere in the Middle East, was much better. For myself, I was a bit knocked up with influenza; so far I had not reported sick, but I intended to do so in the morning. Next day I saw the MO and as my temperature was

99 degrees, he said that I had better come into hospital and see if he could clear up the 'flu.

In the hospital Sister McLaren and Corporal Dickenson were busy fixing a small Christmas tree in the middle of the ward and they also hung red and green streamers from the ceiling. The inside of the ward now began to look very much like Christmas. Squadron Leader Schrenen, the MO, was a huge chap with a very quiet voice. At 10.00 a.m. he came round with Sister Jaques walking behind him. At each patient he asked, 'How are you this morning?' as he turned to take the record card from the Sister. I told him that I had aches and pains all over my body and that I had a very bad cold. That day I remained in bed, listening to the playing of carols over the radio. I eventually turned to a book called *In the Steps of St Paul*, a book that my wife Hilda had sent to me. We heard endless carols over the radio. Bing Crosby sang these carols beautifully and I must say that I spent Christmas Eve very peacefully.

When I woke up at 7.00 a.m. in the hospital I was surprised to find that there was a Christmas stocking at the foot of my bed. The ward orderly told us that at 2.00 a.m. he and the sister had toured the ward, doing the work of Santa Claus giving each man an apple, orange and 25 Players cigarettes. It seems that as they were touring the ward in the stillness of the night, one of the men patients broke his wind very audibly. This made the sister laugh, but the junior medical officer did not flick an eyelid. Additionally, the YMCA sent each patient an apple, an orange, a bar of chocolate, a large bag of boiled sweets, two boxes of matches and 50 Players cigarettes. Christmas dinner in the hospital was a right royal feast. Three special tables were laid down the centre of the ward, and 18 patients sat down to an excellent dinner of soup, luscious turkey served with potatoes and cranberry sauce. We also had a large Christmas pudding, a Christmas cake, fruit and sherbet.

There was but one man in the hospital who was seriously ill and that was a fitter airframes, called Daggers, who was down with pneumonia and said that he did not want to get better. At 6.00 p.m. on Christmas Day the MO had to give him oxygen and after that he began to pick up a bit.

In the afternoon we saw a film show in the main corridor of the hospital. Mr Todd of the YMCA presented *Captain Curious,* a film about the days of sailing ships. There was a lot of rough and tumble in the film, but I came over very tired and went to sleep twice.

After four days in hospital I began to feel better. The MO's treatment had taken the form of a nasal spray, a gargle and two aspirins three times a day, together with one or two inhalations daily, which did me a great deal of good. The MO said that I could be discharged from hospital.

That day we heard that the 26,000 ton German battleship *Scharnhorst* had been sunk off the northern coast of Norway.

As I came out of hospital I met an airman called McBridge, who told me that I had been posted to Penhold 36 SFTS in Alberta, but since this chap was inclined to spread all kinds of rumours I did not take a lot of notice. I went to the Repair Squadron headquarters, where I was told that I was going to Penhold. Apparently some 100 airmen were going away. I had expected that I should be on any repatriation list, but instead I was actually moving another 600 miles west. However, I did feel that I had seen enough of the Estevan area.

That day there came the news that there had been a battle in the Bay of Biscay, where a German ship of 5,000 tons and loaded with war supplies was trying to run the blockade from Japan. A Sunderland flying boat bombed the ship and 11 destroyers were sent out by the Germans to escort the ship in, but three of them were sunk.

Now that I was posted away my energies were concentrated on getting clearance from every section on the station that I was clear of any shortages of kit. Luckily, I had none and soon got clearance.

Now that I was leaving Estevan I ought to mention that the commanding officer of the station caught me out for not saluting him one morning about midsummer. I was walking from the hangar to some place in the camp and as it was a bright sunny day I was wearing tinted sunglasses. I saw a man in battledress uniform approaching towards me, but my mind must have been fixed on something else.

Suddenly this man called out, 'Airman, can you see whilst wearing those glasses? You did not salute me. I am the station commander.'

I quickly said, 'I'm sorry, sir, but I did not recognize you and I had no intention of not saluting you.'

He, too, was wearing sunglasses. I forget now what were his final remarks, but I did not hear further about the lapse.

35

A Posting to Penhold

Monday 3 January 1944 was my last day at Estevan and I had been there for 21 months. I was one of about 50 airmen who were taken by motor transport to Estevan station, or depot, as the Canadians called all stations, and we were put on the 2.45 p.m. train to Moose Jaw. There was quite a little crowd of town folks to see us off. Nobby Clark had a tall and fresh looking girl with him. I thought there might be a few tears, but not so.

Jock Lamb was in charge of our little party of five men who were going to Penhold, and on the train he got so drunk that we had to carry him when we changed trains at Moose Jaw. What a life it was!

We slept overnight in the train to Calgary, and I got into conversation with a Canadian soldier who had been engaged on ground duties with guarding German prisoners of war. He told me several stories of these men. One chap had hidden himself inside a mattress on the day the mattresses were sent to the laundry. Quite by chance a guard looking on noticed that one mattress when thrown onto a truck fell rather oddly, so he prodded it with his bayonet and it jabbed the arm of a prisoner who was attempting to escape. Whilst at Estevan I had heard several tales of how German prisoners had escaped and found their way across the USA to Mexico.

As our train travelled north from Calgary to Penhold there was much snow on the ground, and away in the west we could see the rocky bronze wall of the Rocky Mountains, perhaps 50 miles away.

At Penhold we found that the barracks were all one-storey

buildings with eighty men in each room. The lockers were much smaller than those we had left behind at Estevan and kit-bags had to be hung on the bed frame ends. I had a bottom bed, but as all the kitbags of our party had been lost by the railway people, I had to borrow a blanket from my bed pal. Fortunately, the kitbags turned up intact during the next afternoon.

At work I was allocated to the repair squadron equipped with Oxford aircraft that were powered by British seven-cylinder radial Cheetah engines. My mate was a Cockney chap named Jack Barman, who, in civvy street, ran a transport business in London. He turned out to be a most helpful chap, with adequate knowledge of all the mechanisms of the Cheetah engines and he helped me a great deal. The whole set-up was entirely different from that I had been used to at Estevan. Instead of having to deal almost entirely with the entire overhaul of engines, there were separate sections that took over the repairs of magnetos, carburettors, propellers and so on. At the commencement of an engine overhaul, a chap from one of these sub-sections came over and removed individual items. Sometimes one had to go over and collect a dynamo or other item and I well remember going into one of the separate little workshops and the first thing that I noticed was a postcard that showed a big showman's steam traction engine that belonged to Anderton and Rowland, West Country amusement caterers of roundabouts and so on. The chap who had put the postcard up told me that he, like myself, was a bit of a steam enthusiast and had already visited several Alberta owners of traction engines.

The meals at Penhold were rather better than we had been used to at Estevan. The cooks served the meals very quickly. Long queues soon disappeared. On the second Sunday afternoon we had a very good meal at teatime. There was fried bacon, beans on toast, bread, butter and jam. Here they had a dietician on the station, a married lady who belonged to the WAAFs and it certainly seemed as if she did a good job.

Wing Commander Gifford, our maintenance officer, told me one morning that my recommendation for a commission had been rejected by the chief liaison officer in Ottawa on the grounds that I did not possess sufficient knowledge of motor transport. I entirely agreed with this decision and forgot the whole matter.

On Tuesday 1 February I flew at Penhold for the first time; the trip was in an Oxford aircraft No. 104 upon which our gang had just completed a major inspection. For some reason or other the machine took the air without any of the bumps that we used to experience at Estevan, where the first 500 feet were always a trifle bumpy. From the air we could see the Rocky Mountains quite clearly, whilst the course of the Red Deer river showed up solidly as it passed along a narrow but deep gorge. This was the only flight that I made at Penhold.

One Sunday evening a concert party came to us from Messrs Eaton's Multiple Stores from either Calgary or Edmonton. In this party there were the usual half dozen scantily clad girls. It is pretty awful, when the girls throw up their skirts and show their legs and thighs and the chaps respond with howls of approval. In a public show there has to be some restraint, but at a service performance most things go.

It was my 37th birthday Sunday 12 February 1944, but I had but one person who wished me a happy birthday and I think that he was the only person who knew what the day was to me.

There was not much work in the hangar, so I set about doing a little blacksmithing by making some tube spanners out of ordinary mild steel tubes, which were cut into five inch pieces before drilling quarter inch holes at one end for the insertion of tommy bars. After heating up the end of a tube in the blacksmith's fire, I put the red-hot business end in a vice, placed a hexagon nut over it and hammered it down into the tube, where it soon moulded out into a reasonable fit – and there was your tube spanner. Afterwards I heard that the store's stock of spanners was some 200 or 300 spanners short and a gang of airmen were set to work making spanners that could be classed as scrap and the books squared.

On 18 April we had a big fire in the cookhouse. It seems that around 2.00 a.m. one of the cooks picked up a hot pan full of oil, burnt his hand and dropped the pan. That spilled the hot oil onto one of the fires and up in flames went the bally cookhouse and much of the dining hall. At 5.00 a.m. a flight sergeant came into our barracks to turn out all minor inspection airmen and set them to work on taking tables into the drill hall in order to turn it into a temporary dining hall. The Canadian army depot in Red Deer were phoned and they immediately sent primus stoves and field cookers. Every airman was told to take with him his billy can and tin plate, when at 7.00 a.m. breakfast was served of porridge and bacon ready for us to eat. I thought this emergency work was well done. The cookhouse would certainly be out of use for a week, and probably longer than that.

At Estevan we had to buy the tea that we drank in the hangars at the morning and afternoon breaks of 15 minutes, but this was not so at Penhold. What happened was that one airman went to the kitchen, where he drew a ration of tea and tinned milk which he tipped into a home-made five gallon tank that was put over a primus stove in the cowling bay to boil up. Each gang had an old jam jar that had a wire handle on it. Immediately the 'break' buzzer sounded, the tea was poured out and there was no payment. At Estevan we each had to pay 5 cents for a cup of tea brought round by the YMCA mobile van.

One afternoon early in March, a twin-engined American bomber which the chaps said was a Mitchell plane, landed on our airfield. It had on its wings and body the red star surrounded by a white circle, signifying that it was a Russian plane that America was supplying to Russia on a Lend-Lease basis. It looked to me that the route was over us and then to Edmonton, on the way to Alaska and across the Bering Straits to Russia.

36

Vancouver Island

Although there were many rumours about lists of airmen posted away, and there were several that did come out, only a few men were going back to Great Britain. As the days went past it was obvious that I might as well make use of the time and see a bit more of western Canada. I decided to go over to Vancouver and see what the west coast was like.

On my next 14 days leave I set off to go by the Canadian Pacific Railway from Calgary to Vancouver. The train ride through the Rockies and down by the Fraser River was very interesting. I well remember how the train passed along the rocky river banks, with torrents of water plunging over huge boulders. As we approached Vancouver I noticed that although it was yet early April, most of the trees were already in leaf. One lineside plant of yellowish colour, and very much like our British cuckoo plant, showed up very plainly. A Canadian soldier in the train told me that it was called a skunk cabbage, although as seen from the train it could have been mistaken for a yellow crocus.

I stayed at the United Services Club in Vancouver where my breakfast of cereal and milk, bacon and two eggs, cost me only 25 cents, about one shilling. At 10.30 a.m. I caught the steamboat *Princess Charlotte* for Victoria, where we arrived at about 4.00 p.m. I stayed at the Knights of Columbus Hotel in Victoria. One of my first impressions was that the people of Vancouver Island were pro-British – there were, for instance, Union Jacks flying everywhere. All the beaches around Victoria and Vancouver were littered with huge tree trunks that, having broken loose from timber rafts, were left to rot.

My plan was to hitch-hike up the island, north to the Campbell River. My first lift was given to me by some Canadian soldiers, who dropped me at Duncan after a run of 25 miles. On the way we called upon a friend of these soldiers who had bought a plot of land in the woods for $50.00 and built himself a little wooden house on this plot. This started me thinking that I might do something similar after the war was over. By nightfall I had travelled as far as Nanaimo.

The ride had been through very pretty country with tall fir trees. Here and there we passed farmhouses and practically all of them had a Union Jack flying from its flagpole. I began to feel that I liked Vancouver Island.

At Parksville, which is on the east coast, I went into a hotel called the Rod and Gun Hotel that was run by a lady who asked me where I had come from. She herself formerly lived in Lincoln. She had immediately recognized my Lincolnshire accent and showed me her grandfather clock in the dining hall that had been made by a Horncastle clockmaker.

I was next given a lift by a mechanic of some kind who was on his way to repair a refrigerator at a hotel.

When he asked me what I was doing on Vancouver Island, he immediately said, 'Are you thinking of emigrating to Canada after the war?'

I said that I had no real plans to do so. He then said that with my aero engine experience I could easily pick up the work that his firm did and perhaps I would like to do so. There would be plenty of work of this kind after the war. I told him that I would think about it all. Further on I had a lift in an old army truck, in which the riding was so rough that I hit my head two or three times on the roof. An Irish farmer next gave me a lift. He took me to his farmhouse where he gave me some bread, butter and jam.

After walking several miles between 4.00 p.m. and 8.00 p.m. a prospector named Ed Summers lifted me to his home and gave me a very tasty tea, during which he told me several tales about prospecting for gold.

Eventually I reached the Campbell River where I put up at the Willow Hotel. Next morning I was up at 6.00 a.m. and went with the local postman in his motor delivery van about ten miles, to

Forbes Landing on the Campbell River. All along the route the countryside was bare, with fallen and burnt trees and some gaunt remains of a very big fire that had devastated the area a few years ago. The Forbes Landing Hotel was on the banks of the Campbell River, which at that point was 70 yards wide, and deep, with very clean, clear water. I booked in at the hotel for three or four nights, and found it a most comfortable place.

Mr Forbes, owner of the hotel, let me hire one of his boats and some fishing tackle, so I set off the first afternoon to a lake about a mile from the hotel. The postman had told me the best place in which to fish and in no time at all I caught about three very plump trout, using a spinner that I trolled behind the boat. I had all my fish cooked in the hotel and they were excellent eating.

When I came in from this fishing, a big, fat man, who was a hotel guest, gave me a drink of whisky. I was introduced to a young man named Sylvester, a civilian air pilot who was courting Miss Forbes, who appeared to be an out-of-doors girl who was sociable and attractive. This couple asked me if I would like to join them for a day's boating and picnic. They had a motor boat and, after reaching a long lake, we all sat down to a very enjoyable picnic beside a fallen pine tree, where we ate a selection of sandwiches, cookies and coffee. As I looked around the scene I thought how pretty it all looked, with long lines of pine trees and long, clean beaches of pebbles along the banks of this clear water lake. We tried fishing, but owing to a gusty wind we had no luck. Miss Forbes went off to gather some red-flowering blossoms from wild currants, of which there were many bushes. She was dressed in green gum boots, faded blue corduroy slacks, a khaki windbreaker and a red bandanna. Mr Sylvester wore knee boots for his fishing and a woolly jacket.

From the Forbes Hotel window there was a fine view as one sat at meals. There was a pair of grebes that dived continually for fish. They both dived together and both came up at the same moment. Mr Forbes, who knew the locality very well, told me that there was a logging camp about 12 miles west, so I set out to go and see it, walking about eight miles along the single line private railway that served the camp. I went to a logging party of some Swedish men, who were cutting down trees for which they were paid $14.00, about £3.00, a day. These men had an unusual method of approaching a tree. One man marked with an axe the place where the man behind him should cut through the trunk with his portable power saw – and down came the tree just where they wanted it to fall. They told me that when they had a tree to bring down into a lake the concussion was sufficient to kill several trout, which they took home to eat. The fallen logs, and the men slashed down every tree large or small, had their side branches cut off before being taken to the lake beside the buildings and dropped into the water.

All the men worked very fast. None of the logs was tied with ropes, but just loaded loose on special timber wagons for conveyance by the railway and taken down to the sea at Campbell River. I was told that a train would leave at about 4.00 p.m., when all the loggers rode on it as they went home. I could join them. The locomotives were of Shay-type, with three cylinders vertical on one side, driving a longitudinal shaft that ran below them. This workmen's train was known as 'The Crummy', and it stopped for me to get off at the nearest point to the Forbes Landing Hotel. I enjoyed that day very much indeed.

On the next day, Mr Sylvester and Miss Forbes took me in their car to see the Elk Falls on the Campbell River. The river water fell about 120 feet, where it was overhung by 150 feet high fir trees. Whilst there we saw blue grouse mating, with the cock bird emitting a curious drumming sound.

From the Campbell River I went homewards by bus via the coal mining town of Cumberland, a grubby little town of drab wooden houses. Two men in a car took me 26 miles through what is called Cathedral Grove, where there was a long line of very tall fir trees; one of them was reputed to be no less than 230 feet high. At Port Alberni, which was on the west coast and was a lumber handling place, I stayed in the Bivouac Hotel for servicemen. Together with a corporal who was a pigeon loft keeper with the Royal Canadian Air Force, we were asked to visit a Mrs Tom in the evening. She and her two daughters lived in a nice big house on the Main Street. We found the Toms very pleasant people, who made good conversation about the war situation and how we ought to be able to put the world right. We finished at about

10.30 p.m. with tea and cakes. Somebody or other, probably one of the ladies in the service hostel, happened to tell me that if I wanted to see some of the coastal scenery I should go by the motor boat that went each day up to Ucluelet, where there was a Canadian aircraft base, for the purpose of taking and returning service chaps. I was told that this boat left early, about 7.00 a.m. I think it was, so it was necessary to be up early in the day. To my surprise, there were no charges raised by the boat people; all that one had to do was to be in uniform and go on board. There were no roads to the service station along the coasts. I presented myself and went on board and slept in the saloon for a couple of hours. The run was up the Alberni Canal, as it was called, and which was walled in by high forest of pine trees. Here and there were little settlements with groups of red and green roofed sheds with tall chimneys and perhaps a cottage or two at the rear. I was told that these settlements were fish processing plants that, at the moment, were catching only dog fish for their livers.

At Ucluelet there was a small port with a collection of fishing boats and all of them were crewed by west coast Native Americans.

I had about two hours before the boat returned to Port Alberni, where we arrived back at 4.15 p.m. after a very enjoyable free joyride on the sea.

I spent the following morning at the Alberni waterfront, where a Mr West showed me over the sawmills. A huge crane lifted up big logs from the sea onto a conveyor belt that was part of a lifting device called a rigger. Each log was then picked up in turn by a saw table, as if they were matchsticks. Grips on the saw table held each log by its sides as the table ran past a band saw, forwards and backwards, until the log was ripped into planks. As I looked at this busy, fast and noisy scene, I was left knowing much about how a lumberyard works.

At midday I left for Nanaimo, where I arrived after a 52 mile lift in an army truck. I had found myself holding a fair amount of cash, because people I had met had been so very kind as to give me free meals and so on, so I decided to spend some of it by buying a bit of land. At Nanaimo I was unlucky, because neither the British Legion nor a real estate agent could offer me anything.

I set off south again, and a man named Armshaw, a farmer picked me up, took me to his house, and insisted that I stayed the night with him and his family. In the morning I was taken by the milk delivery van that was collecting milk churns. At one farm about ten quail birds were perched on a low bush and these were the first quails that I had ever seen. When I approached them, the birds promptly flew away. I was dropped down at Duncan.

I found the government office to enquire about buying some land and here I was lucky. I saw a Mr Smythe, who was elderly, with a wrinkled face, but most pleasant and sincere. He said that he could do with an afternoon out of the office and if I could come back at 2.00 p.m. he would run me out to a place called Cowichan Lake, where we could look at several government-owned plots. In the Native American language Cowichan means 'basking in the sunshine'. At Cowichan there was a very big lake that stretched several miles north and there was much lumber work in the area. The place seemed to me very pleasant indeed. At first we looked at one or two small vacant plots on which several new houses were under construction, but when we went down to the Cowichan River I was immediately struck by a riverside parcel of land with a road also running through it. Big trees stood on all this plot, which was bounded on the south by the fast-flowing river and by a CPR single line logging railway on the north. In all the plot comprised about half an acre and there was room for a house to be built on it.

Mr Smythe said, 'Look, you already have three or four wild ducks swimming on the river and in season there are lots of salmon fish that you could catch.'

As we walked over the plot a trunk of a fallen tree lay rotting and, wriggling about on it, there were several small garter snakes. I immediately felt that I would like this plot. I asked Mr Smythe if I could have this bit of land and he said that although he could not conclude a sale he would do what he could with the provincial government in Victoria. He would assess the land as worth

$50.00 and if, as I passed through Victoria, I went to the provincial government offices and discussed the matter with them, they would deal with me.

One of the first things that I did was to go to the Victoria land office, where I was shown to an upstairs room, with its walls taken up by volumes of old books. Two very elderly men dealt with me and one of them pulled down a musty looking large book and looked up the plot of land that I was interested in. He said that the lot was valued at $80.00 and that it was once owned by a lady of some kind or other.

'However,' he said, 'Mr Smythe is our representative at Duncan and he will know exactly the value of the plot that you are after. We will follow the matter up with him and let you know the outcome.' When he saw that my face fell a little at the prospect of further delay, he said, 'Don't worry about it all, because we have millions of acres of land up there,' as he swung his arm towards the north. 'There are only a few Native Americans on this land and we could sell you any amount of it.'

When I asked whether they would like a deposit from me, they accepted the idea, and I handed over $60.00. The outcome of all this was that in about a month's time, I received a letter saying that the plot had been sold to me for $40.00, and enclosing a map on which my land was situated. About 45 years later I decided to sell the land, and I got around $10,000 for it, so I did not do so badly out of the deal.

I spent that night in Vancouver where, after nightfall, I had a walk around the Stanley Park. All around me lay the wide bay of sea, littered with lights. On my right were the big city buildings, all brightly lit, and above them there shone a green light on the chimney stack of the Hotel Vancouver. Away on my left were the lights of the shipyards, busy with the construction of 10,000 ton 'Liberty Ships', upon which work went on day and night. I could hear the sound of the pneumatic hammers. That night I stayed at the Salvation Army hostel for only 25 cents the bed.

First thing in the morning I took the Canadian National train for Edmonton and as we crept along beside the rushing, dirty waters of the Fraser river I thought how pleasant a scene it was.

When we got up into the high Rockies there was snow and ice

everywhere, whilst further on the brown and cheerless prairies of Alberta really did look rather uninviting.

37

Vancouver and Jasper Park

During the last week of January 1944 I managed to make a journey down to Vancouver, travelling down by the Canadian National Railway's 'Continental' express from Edmonton. How I got this leave I do not know, but I went down to the coast. At Jasper Park we entered the Rockies where the Athabaska River leaves the mountains to flow north-easterly and upwards, to empty eventually into the Arctic Ocean. By nightfall we were running down the Yellowhead Valley. One of the trainmen was kind enough to point out Mount Robson, which is 12,700 feet high and the highest point in the Canadian Rockies. The top of the mountain was shrouded in mist and cloud, and everywhere along the line was under deep snow, for it was still midwinter. I slept quite well in the train.

We arrived in Vancouver during heavy rain. A special bus was waiting for us as we got out of the train and it waited ten minutes for us. We caught the 10.30 a.m. steamer *Princess Alice* for Victoria on Vancouver Island and, after passing through many inlets and channels between rocky islets, on which there were many pretty bungalows and houses, we arrived in Victoria. I stayed in the CPR's Empress Hotel in room No. 1 and I must say that this was a very posh hotel. They even made a considerable reduction on the charges for servicemen.

I hitch-hiked the 14 miles north to the famous Butchart's Gardens, provided by the millionaire of that name, and what a delightful garden he had. Around his residence he had in a pine-clothed valley that overlooked the sea. I saw there the arbutus tree, so called because it has red fruits that look like strawberries.

At Brentwood, nearby, I hired a row boat and some rusty fishing tackle and trolled unsuccessfully – although there were several boats with Native Americans in them who appeared to be catching some fish. There were salmon that kept leaping out the water.

In the evening I returned to Vancouver where, in the morning, at the Hudson's Bay Company's shop, I bought a pair of bed sheets for my wife, Hilda. I had been advised to see the Stanley Park and was told that the best way was to hire a bicycle and cycle there. I did this and, in spite of the man who hired the bikes out telling me that the traffic keeps to the right, when I came to the first roundabout I nearly turned left. In the park there were some very tall trees and that was what I wanted to see. One red cedar was almost 18 yards around its base, besides being some 150 feet high. On the following day I again hired a bicycle and from Stanley Park rode over the suspension bridge to West Vancouver. When I stopped to look down from the bridge, I found that it shook with the passing traffic, giving me the feeling that it was unsafe. I went on up a steep hill alongside the Capilano River, to a park that boasts a swing bridge 200 feet above the river. Here there was a small tea shop run by a lady, who made me some tea and gave me two slices of heavily-fruited cake. She had a small wood fire burning and as she talked she threw more logs on to the fire. Outside and down the valley, there were some very tall trees; many of them were cedars. Once again I marvelled that there were such mighty trees in the world.

On the following day I got on to the train for Penhold, but since all or most of the trains did the journey through the gorges up to the Rockies during the night hours, I missed seeing the canyons on the Fraser river stretch of line. As we climbed up the valley of the north Thompson river, the scenery was most picturesque and there was deep snow everywhere.

As the train approached Jasper, the conductor came round so I asked him if I could use my ticket to break my journey in Jasper for one day. He immediately endorsed my ticket for me to do so. I put up at the Athabaska Hotel and before it got dark I walked across the Athabaska River and through the woods to Jasper Park Lodge. Halfway, I suddenly came upon an elk, with her last year's calf, browsing on the twigs of the snow laden trees. Neither of these animals appeared startled or annoyed at my appearance and really the mother elk looked at me with a perfectly harmless look in her eyes. However, I was alone, and did not want to be involved in any argument with an elk that had formidable antlers.

When I came up to Jasper Park Lodge, peacetime haunt of many well-to-do holiday makers, I found that it was now occupied by Scottish ski troops. This place was owned by the Canadian National Railways, and was one of their showpieces.

Next morning I saw from my bedroom window that a wild deer was rummaging in the rubbish bin behind the hotel for any scraps that were left in the rubbish. At 2.00 p.m. I caught the Canadian National train for Edmonton. As we passed along the valley of the Athabaska a high wind blew clouds of sand and dust from the exposed river bed. When the train stopped at Edson I got down for a coffee and a piece of pie. I must say that in all my Canadian travels by train, and in the USA, whenever I ate on the trains or at wayside stations, the food was always first-class. The fruit pies of cranberries, blueberries or cherries were fine fare. I never had a bad lot of eats on trains.

I had just spent seven days on leave, but I do not now know on what grounds it was granted.

38

Alberta Snippets

One could say that Alberta was a greener, better watered province than Saskatchewan. So far as temperature was concerned, a farmer once told me that it was quite as cold, but the periods of extreme frost were shorter than in Saskatchewan. Of wild animals, the variety of them was greater. One day when I was hitch-hiking between Red Deer and Edmonton, I saw a pond that had a fringe of reeds around it and there were heaps of vegetation and mud sticking out of the water. I was told that there was a colony of muskrats in the pond, and that the heaps of vegetable matter contained food that the muskrats had stored up and locally these heaps were called haystacks. From the fact that they were plastered with mud, it would appear that it was a winter store of food. Muskrats are allied to beavers and they have flattened tails similar to beavers.

Whilst travelling on a train to Calgary I sat next to a well-built Canadian soldier who in civil life was a booking clerk on the Canadian National Railway at Jasper. He told me that he had a free railway pass for himself and his wife, given to him after 20 years service, that enabled him to travel on the Western and Central Divisions of the CNR. That was much better than our free travel concessions in Britain.

At that time I was without spectacles, having broken my others, and I had to go to the No. 2 Canadian Wireless School in Calgary to be tested for a new pair. This camp of the Canadian army was stiff with discipline. There were station police in attendance at meals, others were there to see that all airmen were properly dressed and another also to make a check that no knives, forks or spoons were taken from the mess. A big, beefy policeman, a sergeant, came round our living hut to complain that the bed sheets were not turned back the correct eight inches as indicated by two white lines painted on the bed frames. It was a real ritual at the morning break for coffee, and as I went along at just before 10.00 a.m. in the company of a Canadian officer's batman, the orderly sergeant came in and asked us what we were doing there before 10.00 a.m. When we told him that we were on temporary detachment he said no more. The next thing that happened was that two station policemen came in, followed by two fire-fighters, and immediately took up positions to supervise any emergencies. At 10.00 a.m. immediately the wicket gate was opened, a crowd of airmen rushed in from outside. A couple of officers then walked in, and saw that all was going in proper order. At 10.13 a.m. a whistle was blown and everyone made a rush for the door, for everyone must be out of the canteen by 10.15 a.m. Everything at this wireless school worked like clockwork.

At No. 36 SFTS they had a very enviable way of calling meetings in the hangars whenever any changes were proposed to procedures or practices. One of the Flight Sergeants would stand on the balcony of the office and address us as equals. On reflection I think that more might have been done this way at Estevan.

Many Canadians felt that English people were rather stand-offish socially, even with others of their countrymen. To quote an example of this may I mention an incident that occurred when I had a lift from a Canadian in the Sylvan Lake area. He said that on one occasion he had given a lift to an English airman and whilst this man was still in his car he stopped to do some business with a shopkeeper, telling him that he had an Englishman in his car and that he would bring the chap in to speak to him. But when he went out the airman would not get out, saying that he would stay in the car.

The teller of this story told me that he afterwards asked the shopkeeper, 'How do you account for one of your countrymen not getting out, yet you did go out and speak to him?'

'Well,' replied the shopkeeper, 'I suppose that I am an

improved Englishman.'

On the above occasion I had been up to a place called Gull Lake in order to see some fishing through the ice done. A man gave me a lift, saying that he neither drank nor smoked, neither did he mix with loose women. He told me that I should see the man who knew all about the winter fishing, but he took me two miles out of my way and I had to walk back. Gull Lake was about eight miles long and there were men cutting ice that was 30 inches thick. Although there was a hole under a shelter, and I could see the clear lake water underneath, as well as the sandy bottom of the lake, there was no sign of any fish. A man told me that, for some reason or other, the fish had all gone away. Apparently the method of fishing was to dangle a wooden minnow in the water and to spear the fish immediately they struck the minnow bait.

When I got back into Penhold I picked up a letter from my mother, in which she told me that there had been two sets of steam ploughs at work around Barkston. One set had been engaged in the pulling up of trees on Hambledon Hill, and the other had ploughed up some grassland on Dowse's old farm in Honington.

Ever since I came to Penhold there had been many rumours about lists of men for repatriation to the UK. Sometimes, of course, there were such lists, often small but at odd times 20 men could be on their way. But my name never appeared. In any case the times had changed, and it was without doubt that the policy of the RAF was to wind down the Canadian SFTSs.

In mid-March the ice on the Red Deer river started to break up, whilst in Edmonton the ice was also breaking up on the North Saskatchewan river – where there is a marker placed in the river and there is also a sweepstake prize for the correct forecast of time and date of the ice break-up. In 1944 it was 4 April.

In the local newspaper there was an account about a farmer whose well water contained soda, but this was unknown to him. He bought a new drinking trough made of zinc for his pigs. The soda in this water dissolved the zinc and killed 200 of his pigs.

One Saturday evening in mid-February 1944 I took the bus to Red Deer and it was a very cold night with lots of snow on the ground. Whilst listening to the singing of some hymns by members of some Christian society or other, an elderly man in a bearskin coat came up to me to ask whether I would like to go their forces men's recreation centre. I went, but between 8.30 p.m. and 10.15 p.m. they did nothing but sing hymns and a soldier member preached the gospel. At intervals he said that he knew that there were still one or two souls that had not been saved and he implored the men concerned to get up and admit that they had been saved. I am afraid that I found all this soul saving business a bit too much for me, and I got up and went out, making the excuse that I had to catch a bus to Penhold No. 36 SFTS.

There was a small town called Rocky Mountain House, which was about 20 miles west of Penhold. Lots of the airmen went there on drinking bouts, but I went to see what the place was like. There was about 8 inches of snow on the ground, with several groups of men dressed in ten gallon hats, thick woolly jackets and heavy boots, for this was a lumber centre. In the Ritz cafe I sat next to a teenage lumber truck driver on whose jacket was printed the slogan 'There'll always be an England'. He told me that the country west of Rocky Mountain House was still a bit wild, and between us and the Rockies there were bears, timber wolves and cougars.

'Only two days ago,' he said, 'I looked into a bear den under a tree, and there was the old bear right inside sleeping until the spring was really here.'

These bears spend the winter in the roots or rotted stumps of big trees and the female bears actually give birth to their young in those dens.

I noticed that the highway crossed on the ice of the North Saskatchewan River.

On 23 March I was walking through Edmonton on a snowy morning. The whole town looked almost white all over and there was a very cold wind blowing. An old lady stopped me to ask whether I was not cold, saying they, (meaning the forces), should give us better protection against the winter weather.

It made no difference when I told her it was my own fault for I had a Yukon hat in camp, for the old lady went away muttering. 'They should do something better.'

In No. 36 SFTS at Penhold, the work of running the station down had begun to get into its stride. The amount of work on aircraft was much reduced and often we mechanics had little to do. Sometimes we were drafted from gang to gang, or filling for chaps who had been posted back to Britain. At one point I was put on repairing the worn seats used by the pilots on aircraft. On one occasion I was sent to help an airframes fitter to fix some blue celluloid sheets on the inside of front windows of a plane in order to prevent pupils from seeing where they were going instead of flying by their instruments. The chap who was with me soon got tired of this makeshift and difficult job and cleared off after he had done one of these baffles. He was a rather lazy fellow, and usually up to all sort of mischief. For myself, I had never received any training in riveting and it proved a most difficult job to make the aluminium frames that we had made for the celluloid baffles so that they held up on the glass. The next day a warrant officer ticked me off for what he called 'amateurish riveting'.

It had been decided to put some of the planes into storage, so along with two other chaps we were given two Oxford Vs to run up the engines. These planes were fitted with Pratt and Whitney Junior Wasp radial engines with a rated horsepower of 450 h.p. I used the hand-operated self starter on one engine, but it was hard work. The main object of our work was to clear the cylinders of any residues left from the use of leaded petrol, before the engines were put into store. In order to do this we had to use some lead-free petrol. We then forgot to open the petrol cock and we could not restart the engines.

The village of Penhold was quite small. There was a railway station where two or three grain elevators stood beside the railway tracks, and about four or five wooden cottages peeped up behind them. There were, of course, a few large farms with their own farmhouses and each had a large wooden barn. Quite close to the entrance to No. 36 SFTS there was a large farmhouse that let out horses for hire. Several times I joined half a dozen or so airmen for an evening's gallop. The charge for horse hire was very small and I must say that the animals were in good condition.

For some time my nervous system had seemed on edge all the

time, whilst bouts of depression plagued me. The MO tried several sorts of medicine without much effect, so he sent me to see a specialist MO in Edmonton. I went there and reported to No. 4 RCAF Initial Training School, where I saw Squadron Leader Kriener. He asked me a lot of questions, jotting down on a piece of plain paper the answers.

He asked me what work I did in civilian life and when I said that I worked on the London and North Eastern Railway and told him that I had been 18 years in their employ, he said, 'Well I should have thought by that time you would have risen to be the president of the line.'

Squadron Leader Kriener was a youngish officer who had a close-cropped moustache just like that sported by Hitler and, indeed, he had the appearance of Hitler. In the end he said that it was his opinion that once I returned to England I should soon regain my normal health. He would recommend early repatriation and certify that I should not again serve out of Britain.

About a week later, the MO called me in and told me that I had been recommended for early return to the United Kingdom. There was no point in taking any further action; all that I could do was to await events.

When I said that I would like a day off, he said, 'What would you do if I gave you a week's sick leave?'

I immediately replied that I would try and make a trip up the Alaska Highway. About two weeks later I was given leave for seven days.

About a month back, when I was hitch-hiking on the Rocky Mountain House road, I was given a lift by a Russian immigrant who was now a section man, (probably a platelayer), on the C.N Railway. He told me how to catch weasels if they got into woodpiles alongside houses. According to him all that one had to do was to dangle a piece of meat at the edge of the wood heap until a weasel peeped out. Then one had to move the meat out a little, and the weasel reached a little further out showing his head and shoulders. It was then possible, if you knew exactly how to do it, to grab the weasel with the other hand. He showed me the weasel teeth marks on his thick leather mitts. Apparently weasel skins were worth quite a bit of money.

A khaki coloured twin-engined Boston aircraft came in one afternoon and was probably an American machine. It had a tricycle undercarriage that I had not previously seen, whilst it also had an 18 cylinder twin-set of cylinders radial fashion, of the Wright Cyclone type. When the motors were running at idling speed, the whole machine shook with the vibration.

At the same time we had a small high winged monoplane with a single engine, drop down to take away a hospital patient. There was a nursing sister on the plane and the pilot told me that these Norseman planes were much used in the North Country for bush work, as they called it.

Whilst I was at Penhold I did not see much of the Native Americans but I did run into one incident that did not altogether please me, in Red Deer. One very cold winter night, when all the fir tree branches were loaded down with snow, I was booking a room in one of the hotels, when a Native American chief and his squaw came in and asked for a room. They were refused, and had to go away and try elsewhere. Both of these Native Americans were dressed mostly in European clothes and I must admit that the two people had a bit of a smell about them.

During the last two or three months there was an improvement in the war situation. In early April there was an account in the Edmonton newspaper that General Montgomery had addressed troops in Britain, telling them that he was fed up with the war. He asked them to help him finish it off this year. Further, he said that he never put an army into battle unless it had a good chance.

'If we are not sure of ourselves before commencing this second front, we shall not start it,' he concluded.

It seems that for some time there had been fewer air raids on London, but late in April there was a renewal of such air raids. From this I presumed that when I did get back to Britain, I would see more of these night raids. On the other hand there was newspaper advice that the Americans sent a force of 850 bombers to raid Berlin by daylight. They lost 68 four-engined bombers, claiming that at the same time they had shot down 127 German machines during the same operation. To my mind it appeared that both sides had lost a lot of aircraft that they would find it hard to replace.

In Italy, the Germans seemed to be putting up much firm resistance to Allied troops trying to force their way up the west coast below Rome. I am writing this in September 1996, and not long ago a lady came into the same nursing home and she told me that her husband had been an army officer during some of the assaults on the beaches. According to her husband, the Germans had dug foxholes in the beaches, lined them with timber with room for a few men to sleep inside and man the posts 24 hours a day. Immediately our troops landed on the beaches, the German gunners opened a murderous fire on them. She said that it was so dreadful that her husband never forgot it. However, in spite of all these tense situations, we were steadily pushing back the Germans in Italy.

In Russia, the Russian troops had captured Odessa so, all told, we were not doing so badly.

On the night of Friday, 5 May, 1943 we lost one of our Oxford aircraft. After taking off it seemed to vanish, together with a pilot and a trainee pilot. A thorough search was put in hand, aircraft were sent out to search the district and the Americans put up a few of their planes to search the country along the front of the Rockies. There was not a sign of any crashed Oxford. Three days after the take-off the plane was found, with both men dead in it, less than a quarter of a mile outside the Penhold airfield boundary. It had crashed into some low trees shortly after getting airborne. It seemed to me that at Penhold they had more crashes than ever we experienced at Estevan.

It was only about ten days later, whilst I was in hospital, that we had another night crash when a flight sergeant was brought into the hospital after a crash at Bowden. They said that he was terribly badly injured with two broken ankles, a broken leg, his stomach was pushed in, face battered and he had a broken skull.

I stood in the hospital kitchen along with several others and in a few minutes the Padre came out of the ward and said, 'He's gone to God.'

Whilst I was in hospital an under-pilot-training man named Jones came in with suspected mumps or something like that. He told me that in civvy life he had been a detective in the Nottingham county police. He said that a German parachute spy dropped into the arms of a Matlock policeman, and told how women in Liverpool threw some German airmen into the city fires during an air raid. He also said that a 500lb bomb that fell in Sheffield was found to contain nothing but sawdust. This bomb had been made in Czechoslovakia.

39

A Look at the Alaska Highway

On Thursday 11 May the Penhold No. 36 SFTS was inspected by the Air Officer Commanding. This had meant a lot of drills, and the picking of men to be in the party which would be inspected and we also had a high time scrubbing lavatory bowls and so on. I was included in the few hundred men who were to be inspected. In the event I was called into hospital by the MO, who said that he wanted to keep me under observation. In the hospital I had to join in with the cleaning up operations in readiness for the AOC's inspection. One of the jobs given to me was the scrubbing of the kitchen walls in the hospital, followed by giving the lavatory bowls a thorough scrubbing and cleaning.

Actually I was kept in the hospital for 15 days, and this clashed with my plan to have a hitch-hiking trip up the Alaska Highway. In the end, MO Stodley said that I could have a week's sick leave, but when he asked what I intended to do on this leave and I told him that I was to try and have a look at the Alaska Highway, he agreed at once with me. He went on to say that he would like to keep me in the hospital because I was very useful. You see the hospital staff found it extremely difficult to get the 'up' patients to do any work at all.

On Monday 5 June 1944 I went on leave, and set out north for Edmonton. A telegraph fitter gave me a ride to Wetaskiwin and he asked me to go to his home, where we had a very nice supper at the Macdourne home. We chatted rather late, and it was 10.00 p.m. before I booked in at the Salvation army Hostel in Edmonton. There happened to be a Canadian soldier in the bed above mine. He was a Native American who lived at Prince

Rupert on the west coast and was a pleasant enough chap. From him I learned that the second front had started that very morning and that a satisfactory landing had been effected.

My first move in the morning was to go to the RCAF and American air bases at Edmonton, and enquire whether I could have an airlift to Dawson Creek, 500 miles north. There was nothing doing since all available seats in planes were booked up, so I took to the road on my two feet. I soon got a ride with a farmer, who took me 50 miles to Clyde. The country up there was at first flat and marshy, before turning to very rich looking black land, that petered out into a sandy area with lots of small pines growing on it. I had tea along the road, but managed to get to a place called Smith, where a ferry crosses the Athabaska river. The river happened to be in flood and the ferry was not able to operate. There were dozens of cars and trucks standing under the trees awaiting the end of the flood. The small and unpretentious hotel was full and I had to sleep in the lounge, whilst many folks slept in their cars. The landlady of the hotel said that a wolf and a bear had been seen swimming down in the river flood water.

In the morning I had a look at the steel girder bridge that took the North Alberta railway over the 200 yard wide river. This bridge had no foot planking at all, but I managed to cross over. I walked to the place where, upstream, the River Slave ran into the Athabaska river. At this place there was a small boat ferry and the Native American in charge rowed me over. From 11.00 a.m. to 3.00 p.m. I did not see a car or motor truck of any kind, but by a stroke of luck a chap who had turned back from the closed ferry over the river took me to Slave Lake. I put up for the night in the hotel beside the lake. The young Native American woman who was the hotel cook was quite a presentable person, who told me how careful the girls up there had to be with the American soldiers working on the Alaska Highway. Quite a few of these girls had married one of the soldiers, only to find that they already had a wife in the USA.

After tea somebody or other said that an evening boat trip had been arranged on the lake, to go to the house of a German hunter named Ehren. I went with the party and we found a large wooden house on an island, where this German and his young wife lived.

There was one very large room and it was a veritable museum of wild animals' heads and antlers, far too many for my liking. Anyway, these Germans made us very welcome. As we went back we passed hundreds of wild duck swimming on the water and somebody in the party shot one of these ducks, which we picked up and took with us.

All about this north country there are large areas of what is called muskeg land, that is covered with boggy grassland growing little but small pine trees. In fact, it is just an uninhabited wilderness. There are, however, many pretty views from Slave Lake, which is 74 miles long and 14 miles wide. A great deal of commercial fishing is done, using stationary nets into which the fish swim and are held by their gills in the mesh of the nets.

From Slave Lake to Grande Prairie it is some one hundred and twenty miles. At evening next day I was still stuck on the road and a very lonely country it was. A car did in the end pick me up and it did land me at about 10.00 p.m. in Grande Prairie.

On the following morning I made up my mind to reach Dawson Creek that day if at all possible; it was a trip of about 150 miles west. It seemed as if, for the greater part of this trip, I had been riding in the back of 10 c.w.t. trucks, over roads that were very bad for travel. When I first left Edmonton, the roads were very little more than plain earth, but as I got further north the roads became even worse and in some places they were little more than hard grass tracks with humps and bumps in them. There were also fairly deep ruts in places, that let the truck wheels slip down, and the bottom of the truck hit the ground with a bump. It was surprising, though, to find that the truck and car drivers made good timing. At a place called Wembley there were five grain elevators and I was told that much wheat was grown in the locality, although this was just about the northern limit at which it could be grown. I believe that there are also other northern limits at which various other crops can be grown, but, strangely enough, in every instance the quality of the crops is top class. On this particular day of spring, the farmer's wheat was coming up through the ground very nicely.

I had intended taking the train to Dawson Creek, but a Vancouver man picked me up in his motor truck and whisked me off there. It was about 4.00 p.m. when we reached Dawson Creek, which is the southern end of the Alaska Highway. The Northern Alberta railway terminates here, and the Alaska Highway begins. Goods are taken by rail up to Dawson Creek, whence they are put onto trucks and taken up to Alaska. I stayed overnight in the Condill Hotel in Fort St John and from the hotel bedroom I could see the clouds of dust flying up from the traffic on the Alaska Highway. The highway is surfaced with loose gravel and is 50 yards wide. At St John I tried to get an airlift from the Canadians, but they could not help at all because all available plane seats for Edmonton or further up the highway were booked. When I went over to the American air base I was told to hang around a bit in case a seat on one of their planes became available.

I decided to press on up the highway and hitched a further 50 miles north. The country through which the highway passed was well-wooded and I passed by a small plantation of poplar trees upon which a host of caterpillars had descended and eaten off every bit of the new spring leaf. I never saw anything like that, where trees had been stripped of every leaf. One thing that also surprised me was the absence of much traffic that day on the road. It was a lovely day as I walked along the highway and soon I was aware of a most delightful scent in the air. I came across a house in the trees by the roadside and went over to it and bought a glass of milk. At the same time I noticed how the ground under the trees was carpeted with dwarf wild roses. It was the scent of these pink flowering wild roses that filled the air so fragrantly. A little further on I heard the sound of a sawmill in the trees and I thought that perhaps here there would be a steam engine for me to see – but they had an oil engine to power their large saw bench.

A big tall lumberman came up to me asking, 'Where are you off to, fellow?' When I told him who I was and what I was doing, he immediately said, 'We have just stopped for a meal, will you come in and have what you like to eat? We have plenty of flapjacks, pancakes to you, with maple syrup.'

I accepted, and we walked into the small dining section, and I had a very good meal indeed. When I offered to pay for what I had eaten, they all just laughed at me. Really these Canadians are most generous people.

It was Saturday 10 June and I went a little further up the highway, but rides were not very forthcoming. I did get picked up by a timber lorry driver, but his lorry broke down. This driver was able to put the gear into bottom and then switch on the self-starter and that was powerful enough to move the truck off the road. The driver then said that he thought I had better go back to Fort St John as soon as I could; he knew where he could phone for assistance. I went back, and that was the farthest north that I got on the Alaska Highway.

Generally speaking, the countryside along the highway was quite pretty, although there was not any sight of the Rockies on the section that I travelled over. How far the road went before it passed out of Canadian territory I never knew.

I read in a local newspaper that only one life had been lost in the making of this road. A black man in the American army was driving a truck that broke down and he got out and lit a fire, but left it to walk back 14 miles to his base and was frozen to death. You see the temperature was down to −50F and he had no chance of survival.

At Fort St John I went back to the US air base and enquired about the chances of an airlift. They said that there was a plane expected during the night and they put me up in a little wooden barrack hut fitted with a telephone. If there was a place for me they would phone me. At about 4.00 a.m. they did ring me up, saying that I should get up and come immediately to the guardroom. I was given a written pass that allowed me to fly down to Edmonton. I chatted with the US chaps for some time and from what they said sergeants were used to do the work of engine maintenance that I had been doing in the RAF.

Eventually a big twin-engined C57 plane came in. Along with 16 other fellows and two tons of freight, we took off for Edmonton. The plane was painted white, with a silver star on its fuselage. During the flight the going was rather bumpy. We passed over lots of barren-looking country. On the journey I did not feel too well and several of our passengers were air sick. The journey of 400 miles was covered in just over 3 hours. We landed with a bump at Edmonton and found that we had burst a tyre.

When I got off the plane nobody asked me who I was or what I was doing and when I asked a US airman where the gate was, he said, 'Have you had a meal?'

He then insisted that I should go straight into their canteen or dining room and help myself. He would not hear any excuses of mine that I was nothing to do with the US forces and so on.

He went with me, and together we entered the mess, where the first thing that I saw was about two buckets full of delicious strawberries, and all that he said was, 'Help yourself.'

I had a splendid Sunday afternoon tea. Once again, may I say how wonderfully generous these Yanks were.

I went to the Salvation Army hostel in Edmonton and stayed that Sunday night. At around 8.00 p.m. on Monday night I got back into Penhold No. 36 SFTS, and almost immediately I was told by an acquaintance that my name was on a draft that was posted back to the United Kingdom.

I reckon that my trip up to the Alaska Highway had amounted to 700 miles hitch-hiking, and about 400 miles by air. This was not bad going.

40

Homeward-bound

Now the time had come when, after two years and two months in Canada, I was at last on my way home. Really, the time had, in the main, passed along reasonably quickly. At times it seemed that it was only two or three weeks since I arrived in Canada.

I wrote my 167th letter to Hilda, my wife. I did not mention that I was on my way home, because I thought that it would be a little surprise for her. I packed up all my belongings, and found that someone had pinched my skates.

On Thursday 15 June 1944, the commanding officer of No. 36 SFTS came after lunch to say goodbye to the 23 fellows who were leaving for the UK. He reminded us of the good times that we had spent together at the 'Buffalo' and other places. I thought that he had taken a little drink with his lunch, but it was kind of him to come and say goodbye. Pete Fowler, one of the chaps going back to Britain, had lost a shovel and our departure was held up half an hour whilst clearance for it was obtained from the stores side. Anyway, the train was late, and at 5.00 p.m. we were on our way, via Calgary.

Jack Ackroyd, Jenkins, Bert Grant and myself were in the same coach on the train. We each had a sleeping berth. I had a lower bunk, where a good lot of soot and cinders from the steam locomotive in front blew into the compartment. As I looked out of the window whilst the prairies went past, I could see that the recent rains had coloured up the fields into a pale green. There was also a lot of wild mustard that was shown up by its yellow flowers.

On the second day we reached Winnipeg about 6.45 p.m. and

by nightfall we left the prairies and came into country that had lots of low bushes on it.

At night a black trainman came round to pull out our beds and in the morning he came round and packed up. Eventually our trans-Canada train reached the rocky north shore of Lake Superior. At times we had long views south over this lake, which is the largest lake in the world. From daylight until noon the train passed along the north shore of the lake.

At Ottawa the river looked wide and shallow and the country around was pleasant enough. The parliament building stands on a rock above the river on its east bank. There was a canal with five or six locks just below the parliament building. The whole area presented a pretty setting. The soils around this part of Canada appear to be of shallow depth and few people live hereabouts.

At 8.00 p.m. the little black trainman came and made up my bunk bed and what a treat it was to lie abed and watch the Canadian countryside pass back along the coach windows. Between Ottawa and Montreal there is a great deal of wild sumac bush. In Montreal the train stopped for three hours, so three of us walked into the town where we popped into the Roman Catholic cathedral whilst the morning service was in progress. There were many people here who spoke French, but I did not care about the city itself. As we left, the train passed over the St Lawrence river which is, there, a quarter of a mile wide. Each day we took our meals in the dining car.

On Monday 10 June 1944 we were told that we must get up at 4.00 a.m. in order to take early breakfast at 5.00 a.m. because we should reach St Johns at 5.00 a.m. where the train stops. I think that St Johns is the dirtiest place that I have seen in North America. There are grubby buildings much as one might see in Grantham or Newark. In the harbour there was an Irish steamer, with neutrality marks all along its sides for the benefit of German submarine crews.

It was 11.00 a.m. before we reached Monkton, where we had to march through the town to the RAF reception centre. This was the end of our four day rail journey across Canada.

At Monkton we began the process of handing in much of our winter Canadian clothing. We also had a kit inspection, when worn clothing and uniform were changed for a reasonable dress to go home with. I made a little hole in the seat of my trousers in order to get a new pair.

During Thursday afternoon an officer asked for two dozen volunteers to work in the base. Only 12 came forward, and this made the officer furious.

'Who do you think you are? Is this typical of the RAF?' he asked. He continued, 'You fellows have had a long holiday in Canada whilst other chaps have been giving their lives in France.' A second appeal was made and another dozen chaps came forward and, turning to us all he said, 'Those who have volunteered can have the afternoon off – the 600 others will work.'

There had been rumours of our going home on the *Queen Elizabeth* from New York, but we were told that on Sunday we should leave Monkton for a sailing, but we were not told which boat or from which port.

As we were close to the Fundy Bay, in which there was at times a very high tidal wave or bore that comes up the Petite Zodiac River a few miles to the east of us, I went to see if anything was worth seeing, at around 1.00 p.m. That day there was a low wave across the river about two feet high. At its best this tidal wave can pile up to 20 feet.

On our last afternoon we were all given a half day off. I used it to go into town and buy, at Eaton's Store, two enamel saucepans and some groceries, for we all knew that many small items such as these would be in short supply in Britain. Later on that day I walked about five miles south, to a little village the name of which I did not note. All along the roadside there were lots of wild strawberries that were very good to eat. I began to think that I liked this part of Canada.

Next morning we all had to be on parade, with all our kitbags and so on. We were told that we should leave by train, without telling us more than that we were heading for a boat home.

There was much talk, however, that we were off to Halifax. In the end we landed up at Halifax and the train stopped alongside a fairly large steamboat named *Nieu Amsterdam*, which I imagined was a Dutch vessel that had been used in peacetime for passenger travel.

At about 11.00 a.m. we set out from port on what was a slightly foggy morning and the first thing that was said to us was that we should not talk on deck, because German submarines had been known to surface and their crews listen to get a bearing on ships. The boat was very crowded and I had a corner in what was probably the dining or drawing room of the ship. As I lay in my bunk under the ceiling, I had a plaster cherub of some sort looking down at me from one of the ceiling decorations. As soon as we set off, I could see that we had no escorting vessels, nor did any appear for the rest of the voyage, but the ship was quite a fast runner and I expect that it was capable of outpacing German submarines.

The cooking on board was not of first-class quality. I could not eat the newly cooked and leaden bread. Most of the chaps, like myself, had diarrhoea and there were long queues for the few lavatories.

The weather was rather dull and cold on the Atlantic; everybody was looking for some corner in which to shelter. And really the ocean looked so vast that it did seem a great waste of water. Here and there we saw porpoises and once a whale surfaced almost alongside us, before it dived again in two spouts of water. We did not see many birds at sea, there were no seagulls, and all that we saw in mid-Atlantic were small swallow-like seabirds. To my amazement we did not have to have drills in case of submarine warnings, so it did seem that we had got the upper hand of the Germans at the moment. On Sunday 2 July 1944 we ran into shoals of porpoises and soon we came up to a whole fleet of ships, anchored in a long line and everything was quiet and peaceful. For some reason or other our ship belched out a great cloud of black smoke.

We had to disembark later that day in the middle of the Clyde and were taken ashore by open motor boats. How small the railway carriages looked, also the goods wagons.

But we were back in Britain.

EPILOGUE

Back to the Job

We went to West Kirby in Cheshire for a few days and were then put on a special train for London. When I reached Cambridge I went into the office of the railway control where they phoned the loco foreman at March that I was on my way home and would they send word round to my wife Hilda that she might meet me at the station? They did so and Hilda was at the station with her bicycle to meet me. She was very pleased to see me all in one piece.

I had two weeks leave, so we went to Norfolk for a few days. We got to King's Lynn, only to be told that we had come into a restricted area without permission. The station ticket collector said that the best thing we could do was to take a night's stay in a home near the station and then get out of town immediately after breakfast.

There was not much in the way of enemy bomb damage to be seen, but the town of March had several houses knocked about. They were near the railway, so it was obvious that the German airmen had been aiming at the railway yards.

It seemed to me that, as I met old acquaintances, they were mostly fed up with the war and looked forward to its end. Folk were getting tired of the same old plain food and not being able to go on holidays. To me, after America, it was obvious that everybody looked rather shabbily dressed. The railways were getting into a run-down state, the locomotives were dirty and never got cleaned.

One Peterborough locomotive man that I chanced to meet said to me, 'If the Germans had been faced with running our railways, they would have lost the war long ago.'

At the end of my overseas service entitlement to leave I was sent to Warboys aerodrome near Ramsey, where they had Lancasters and some Mosquitos. The hangar floors were half an inch deep in oily muck and were never swept up, but the work of repairing the planes went on.

Later I was sent to Whyton aerodrome, where some of the Lancaster planes operated with the Pathfinder Force headed by Air Vice Marshal Bennett. All the work that we did was to repair the famous Rolls-Royce Merlin engines. These engines were noted for the performance that they gave. The work may have been dirtier than in Canada, but we did not have the strict discipline to contend with. I enjoyed my days at Warboys and at Whyton.

In the autumn of 1945 I was demobbed and after four weeks leave I went *back to my job on the railway at March*.

At the time of writing in 1997 I thought I had finished, but by a stroke of luck I got in touch with Gregory Cliff Salmers MLS, the librarian of Estevan Public Library. He has given me some very useful information about what happened to No. 38 Service Flying Training School. On 11 February 1944 the Royal Air Force decommissioned the airfield. About a week previously a special train took the RAF personnel to Montreal enroute for a boat to Britain. The CO and another officer left shortly afterwards.

In the Estevan graveyard are the graves of the 12 RAF airmen who died of either accident or illness. Each grave is marked with one of the standard metal plates. There is also a brass memorial plate at Estevan church commemorating the 12 men. Fourteen Estevan girls married young RAF men and no fewer than 13 followed their husbands overseas.

After the RAF left, the buildings were used for a variety of purposes, such as storing aircraft, and two hangars were, after the war had ended, loaned to the municipality of Estevan for a civilian flying school. Eventually a new municipal airport was built north of Estevan town.

Today, the whole site, except for the runways, has been cleared. The ground has been sold to a Canadian mining company who intend to mine the coal that lies below.